Stock Market

(2 Books in 1)

John James

Published By: John James

Copyright © All rights reserved

No part of this publication may be copied, reproduced in any format, by any means electronic or otherwise, without prior consent from the copyright owner and publisher of this book.

Stock Market Investing:
The Complete Beginner's Guide to Gain Passive Income by Stock Market Investing

Introduction 8
Chapter 1: The Right Mindset Makes All the
   Difference 10
Chapter 2: Picking Out Stocks to Invest In 17
Chapter 3: How to Purchase Stocks 27
Chapter 4: What Options Do I Have For Stock
   Market Investing? 32
Chapter 5: Picking Out Your Investment Strategy .. 42
Chapter 6: Different Styles That Expert Traders
   Use for Stock Trading 57
Chapter 7: Rules That Help to Reduce Your Risks
   When Investing in the Stock Market 66
Conclusion 77

Options Trading:
The Complete Guide to Trading Options table of Contents

Introduction 82
Chapter 1: Understanding the Options Trade 86
Chapter 2: How The Options Trade Works in Real-Life Scenarios 92
Chapter 3: Understanding the Call Option 96
Chapter 4: Understanding the Put Option 101
Chapter 5: Components of an Options Trade 105
Chapter 6: Understanding the Moneyness of Options 108
Chapter 7: Assessing the Moneyness in Call Options 114
Chapter 8: Assessing the Moneyness in Put Options 118
Chapter 9: Understanding the Premium 122
Chapter 10: Understanding Intrinsic Value 125
Chapter 11: Understanding Time Value or Extrinsic Value 129
Chapter 12: Understanding Time Decay 131
Chapter 13: How an Actual Trade Takes Place 134
Chapter 14: Closing an Open Call or Put Option Position before the Expiration Date 140
Chapter 15: Valuation of Options in the Bullish and Bearish Markets 144
Chapter 16: Understanding Open Interests (OI) in Options 151
Chapter 17: Understanding the Greeks 155
Chapter 18: Understanding Delta 158
Chapter 19: Understanding Gamma 160
Chapter 20: Understanding Theta 162
Chapter 21: Understanding Vega 166
Conclusion 168

Stock Market Investing

The Complete Beginner's Guide to Gain Passive Income by Stock Market Investing
(Learn Secret Hints and Tips to Make Your Money Work for You!)

© Copyright 2018 by John James

All rights reserved.

The following eBook is reproduced below with the goal of providing information that is as accurate and reliable as possible. Regardless, purchasing this eBook can be seen as consent to the fact that both the publisher and the author of this book are in no way experts on the topics discussed within and that any recommendations or suggestions that are made herein are for entertainment purposes only. Professionals should be consulted as needed prior to undertaking any of the action endorsed herein.

This declaration is deemed fair and valid by both the American Bar Association and the Committee of Publishers Association and is legally binding throughout the United States.

Furthermore, the transmission, duplication or reproduction of any of the following work including specific information will be considered an illegal act irrespective of if it is done electronically or in print. This extends to creating a secondary or tertiary copy of the work or a recorded copy and is only allowed with express written consent from the Publisher. All additional rights reserved.

The information in the following pages is broadly considered to be a truthful and accurate account of facts and as such any inattention, use or misuse of the information in question by the reader will render any resulting actions solely under their purview. There are no scenarios in which the publisher or the original author of this work can be in any fashion deemed liable for any hardship or damages that may befall them after undertaking information described herein.

Additionally, the information in the following pages is intended only for informational purposes and should thus be thought of as universal. As befitting its nature, it is presented without assurance regarding its prolonged validity or interim quality. Trademarks that are mentioned are done without written consent and can in no way be considered an endorsement from the trademark holder.

Introduction

Congratulations on downloading this book and thank you for doing so.

The following chapters will discuss everything you need to know to get started with investing in the stock market. While some people will choose to start their own businesses, work on their retirements, or work in real estate investing, there is nothing that works as well, and provides the return on investment, as when you work in the stock market.

This guidebook will talk about everything that you need to know to get started with investing in the stock market. We will talk about the mindset that you need to see success with the stock market investment, how to pick out stocks that will provide a good return on investment, how to enter the stock market, how to pick good strategies, and how to reduce your risk. Whether you have been an investor in the past or not, this guidebook will help you to get started in the stock market.

There are plenty of books on this subject on the market, thanks again for choosing this one! Every effort was made to ensure it is full of as much useful information as possible, please enjoy!

Chapter 1

The Right Mindset Makes All the Difference

When it comes to investing your money and putting it to work for you, there are several opportunities that you can choose from. Each person has their own personal style when it comes to these investments and picking out the one that is best for their needs. Some people might like to get their hands dirty and follow the market with real estate investing. Some like to play it safe and will just put their money into a retirement plan. And others will choose to work with the stock market.

Often it will depend on how much time you have to devote to the investment, how much money you can put towards the investment, and how much risk you are willing to take. Of course, the more risk you are willing to take, the more money you could potentially make. There is also the risk of losing more money, which is why you need to find the perfect balance between how much you can earn with an investment and how much you could lose with that investment if things go wrong.

While there are a lot of different investment opportunities that you can choose from, such as real estate investing, investing in bonds, starting your own business and more, you can also work with the stock market. This type of investment will include you taking your money and investing it to help another company grow. In return for investing in a company that does well, you will earn dividends each quarter, or part of the profit that the company brings in. Or you could get into the process of buying the stocks at a lower price and selling them when the price goes up so that you can make a profit.

Those are the two most common ways to make money in the stock market, but there are many others that you can work with as well. With all the options available for investing in the stock market, it is no wonder that a lot of people choose to go with this option. You will be able to take a look at how much time, money, and risk you have available and choose which stocks, as well as which strategies, will be the best for you. Depending on which stocks you go with, it is even possible to start making a profit without all the wait.

It is exciting to get into the stock market and see how things can go for you, but some people want to weigh all their options and make sure that they can actually make money rather than losing out on money. When you are ready to start entering the stock market, and you want to make a good income from your investment, make sure to learn the right strategies that will ensure that you see success.

Starting off in the stock market

Before you decide to jump right into stock market investing, you must take some time to determine what your goals are for doing this kind of investing. If you jump into this investment without thinking it through, you will fail miserably. You should know where you want to start out at as well as why you are doing the investment. Do you want to start investing to help your retirement fund, to make a side income, or even to replace your full income? The answer to this will help determine how you will behave when you get into the market.

There are many options that you can choose for goals when you want to invest. Choosing the right one can sometimes help you to figure out how much risk you want to take and which stocks you want to invest in. For example, if you are looking to turn the stock market investment into your full-time income, you may be willing to take on more risk to bring in more money. If you want to make just enough to put some in the bank or pay off a few bills, then it may be best to go with less risky options.

No matter which goal you choose for investing, you will quickly find that the stock market is one of the best options that you can choose for your investment. There are many companies that you can choose to work with, many strategies that work well, and even different levels of risk that you can pick from. You can pick a plan that has a bit more risk that will also help you earn more rewards, or you can take your time to learn more about the stock market and pick less risky options while still making money.

You do need to have a good idea of how the stock market works and how to get into the game before you start. First, we need to understand what a stock is. A stock is a type of security that will give the investor, or you if you choose this option, part ownership in the business that the stock belongs to. This also means that the investor will be able to claim some of the assets and earnings of the business as well. The buyer will be known as a shareholder, and along with some of the other investors, they will be the new owners of that business. The amount of ownership that you have will depend on a number of stocks that you possess. There are also two types of stocks including common stocks and preferred stocks.

How do I trade in stocks?

One of the first questions that you may have as a new investor is how to trade stocks. When you join in on the stock market, you must trade stocks using the stock exchange. This is simply the place where the sellers and buyers of stocks will come together and then agree on the price for a particular stock. There are a few places where you can physically go to do this, but for the most part, you will do your trades online.

Once you get into the stock market and look at it for a bit, you will notice that the prices of each stock will change all the time. Many different factors come into play when determining what the price of the stock will be. These factors change on a regular basis, which is what makes it so hard to keep the prices steady for the long term. For example, if the supply of the stock is pretty high while the demand is low, the price of that stock will stay lower. If the demand for the particular stock goes up and the supply goes down or stays the same, then the price of those stocks will go up as well. The prices of the various stocks will usually be what people in the stock market see as the worth of the stocks and can show how interested people are in purchasing that stock at one time or another.

Not only can you pay attention to the demand and supply of a particular stock, but you will also find that the earnings of the company behind the stock can determine how much it is worth as well. This means that you need to look at how much money the company is able to earn each year. Of course, the exact amount will change from one year to another, so it is a good place to start to see if the company is growing and if you will be able to make some money from the investment. It is easy to find these numbers by looking through some of the financial journals and reports that the company is required to put out in order to be on the stock market.

Keeping track of all the prices on the stock market can be hard, and the fact that there are a lot of reasons that these stock prices will change can be a hassle as well. You have to look at some of the changes that the company has recently made or will make soon. Addtionally, you need to look at how well the economy is doing at the time. What this all means is that you do need to do some research. Those who just jump right into the stock market and don't pay attention to what is going on around them are more likely to fail and lose a lot of money.

There is no rush when getting into the stock market. You can do this on your own time and do some thorough research to make sure you are picking out the right stocks and not just risking everything. Finding a good stockbroker to help you along the way can make the process so much easier as well.

Chapter 2

Picking Out Stocks to Invest In

After taking some time to research the stock market and what it has to offer, it is important that you take the time to pick out the right stocks. There are thousands of companies available on the stock market, but not all of them will provide you with a good return on investment. Some will provide you with one of the best opportunities to make money without all the risk and others will be failures right from the beginning. As a beginner, you may be worried about how you will sort these out so that you can pick the right stocks to make the most money for you.

The first thing that you should look at when you are ready to join the stock market is that you should never just pick out a stock, no matter what the circumstances are, simply because you heard through the grapevine or from a friend of a friend that the stock was a good one. Doing your own research is important. You can take the advice of other people, such as friends who are in the stock market and your broker, but remember that this is your investment and you need to be the one in control of it. Do some of your own research on the market, and you will soon learn which stocks are the best ones for your needs, regardless of what other people say.

If you have already done some research and have come up with a list of companies that you want to look at some more and possibly invest in, make sure to take some time searching on their website. Most of them will have information about their stocks, and this can be helpful when making your decision. You need to take a look at all of their reports on finances if possible to because this tells you how the company has done so far on the market. You will be surprised at how much information you are able to get about a company just by snooping around a little bit.

While there are a lot of things that you will need to consider when it comes to picking out a stock to work with, you need to go with one that will actually make you money in the process. Never pick a stock that is obviously going to cost you more than you can earn and try to go with the ones that are winners. There are a few things that you can take a look at to limit your risks including:

- The margin of profit for that company.
- The debts that a company has and how much those debts are.
- The return on equity with that company.
- The debt to equity ratio. This is a good thing to look up because it will give you an idea of how this particular company spends their money and whether they do so responsibly or not.
- How the company has done in the past and whether they are expected to do the same, better, or worse.

What should I be looking for?

So, you may be curious about what things you need to look for to pick out a good company to invest in. You will want to spend some time looking through charts and graphs to see how a particular stock has been doing inside the stock market, but that is only one part of the story. You also need to take a look at the company itself to see if it will maintain that status for the long term. For example, there may be a company who looks good when you go through the charts and graphs, but if they are not good at spending money or keeping their debts down, then they are not the company for you. Some of the different things that you should consider looking at when you are ready to pick out a stock includes:

Who manages the business

This is one of the first things that you should look at when you want to start investing in a company. Who manages the business will help you to figure out how the company is doing now as well as how it will do in the future. Many beginners consider the management of a company not all that important. However, if the current management is not doing well with running the company, even a solid company can go downhill fast.

Now, you need to carefully consider the management of a company before you decide to invest in it. There are a few points that you can consider such as what the return on equity is if the shareholders are still earning a profit each year. If the equity return of the company is five percent or higher, it is usually a safe bet that the company will keep growing and doing well. Also, look and see how the management is doing with others and with each other. Are they getting along and making decisions that are good for the company, or is there are a lot of internal fighting that could ruin the company?

Pick a sector that is doing well

When you are picking out stocks, it is important that you find some that come from a business sector that is also doing well. Depending on how the economy is doing, it is possible that some industries will still do well in a downturn, or at least some industries will do better than the rest. There are also times when the economy is doing well, but one or two industries are not doing as well as the rest of the market.

This is why it is so important to pick out industries that are doing well. You may also want to consider spreading your money out a bit so that you can avoid trouble if one of your industries starts to do poorly. And, while it is best to go with industries that are predicted to do well over a long period of time, if you find that one of your industries is not performing the way that you want, it is easy to sell that stock and try something else.

Growing profits

You also need to look for a company that is making profits. If you see a company that is losing money from the start, then it will be hard for you to get a good return on investment. You also want to make sure that the company is getting bigger profits each year. When the company keeps on growing their profits, it is doing well and has a lot of popularity that is growing as well. This makes it a good investment option for many people. The bigger the profits, the better return on investment you will be able to get.

The size of your company

Some investors want to work with a company that is a little bit smaller. They think that these are easier to work with and that they will be able to monitor that company a little bit better than some of the bigger companies. However, there have been some studies done that show how smaller companies will actually carry more risks with them compared to investing in some of the bigger companies.

The reason for this is that a lot of the bigger companies have taken their time to become established. They didn't become big overnight, so you know that they will be safe investments. As a beginner who has never worked in the stock market, it is usually better to go with a company that is bigger and more established. After you have learned how to work in the stock market and you understand the types of risks that you want to take, you can choose to go with a smaller company if you would like.

Also, as a beginner, you should make sure that you are avoiding penny stocks. These sometimes are tempting because they are usually really inexpensive to work with. However, these companies are really risky and often they do not need to provide users and investors with financial information even though they are on the exchange. It is likely that you will lose a lot of money if you choose to work with these penny stocks. It is a better idea to stick with one of the main companies that are on the stock market so that you know they are safer options and you are more likely to make money.

Look at the dividend payments

When you look at a company, check and see if they are able to pay out dividends to their investors. Companies that are able to share their profits already are great options for a beginner to work with. This shows that the company is already able to manage their debts while still sharing the profits with the shareholders. It is likely that they will be able to do it again and you will continue to receive these payments in the future.

Also, when you are deciding how much you can make with dividend payments, you should go with a company that is able to pay you at least two percent. This is a good sign that the company is pretty steady and that you will be able to make a decent amount of money each year. If you can find one that is higher than the two percent, then you are able to make even more in profits.

Manageable debt

While you are taking a look at some of these companies to invest in, you should take a look at the debts that they have. The company doesn't necessarily need to be completely debt free, but they need to have a good balance between the amount of debt that they take on and the amount of profit that they are able to bring out.

There are some good debts that a company will have, especially if they are just starting out or if they have recently undergone an expansion. They may have some debts for their buildings, for their equipment and so much more. You are not likely to find a company that doesn't have any debt, but you should look for one that has kept their debt manageable for the profits that they make each year. If you are looking for a company and they have so much debt that they are barely able to cover it each month, then it is best to go with someone else. In this case, it is unlikely that they will be able to keep managing that debt and you will lose money.

Go with liquid stocks

And finally, another thing that you can consider when you are looking at stocks to invest in is how liquid those stocks are. Liquid stocks are good because these are the ones that you will easily be able to find sellers and buyers for. If you go with a stock that is not liquid, you may find that it is really hard to sell that stock later on when you want to leave the market. Most stocks will have some kind of liquidity with them, but the more liquid the stock is considered, the easier it is for you to sell it when you would like.

Try to find a stock that has a happy medium. You want it to be at a good price, so you do not want the demand for that stock to be too high. If the demand is too high, it will be too expensive to get ahold of it to start. But the demand needs to be high enough that when you are ready to leave the market, no matter what that reason is, you will be able to find someone who is willing to purchase the stocks from you.

There are a lot of things that you will need to consider when it comes to picking out the right stocks for your needs. You should do your research to figure out who is managing the company, how they are doing with their profits and their debts, and find stocks that will be easy to sell if you decide to leave the market. When you are able to do this, you are sure to find some good and secure stocks that will help you to make a good profit.

Chapter 3

How to Purchase Stocks

Earlier, we took some time to explore the things that you should look at to find the perfect stocks to invest in. You want to make sure that you pick out stocks that will actually bring you money, ones that have good management, steady profits, and manageable debts so that you can make money. After you have done some research on the stock market, it is time to enter the market and actually purchase the stocks that you want to invest in. Let's take a look at how you enter the market by purchasing stocks.

Use a broker

Since you are a beginner and you have not had the opportunity to work in the stock market yet, it may be a good idea to work with a broker. The broker will help you make smart decisions when it comes to the stocks that you should invest in. Brokers spend their time learning how to work with the market, and they have been doing work in this industry for many years. They have a lot of experience and expertise that is needed to help you make good decisions. Beginners can really benefit from taking the advice from a broker they trust.

There are actually a few types of brokers that you can choose to work with and it will depend on how much you would like to spend on the broker and how much advice you will end up needing. The first broker that you can work with is a full-service broker. This type of broker will be responsible for managing all of the stocks and purchases that happen on your account. You will be able to consult with them about any purchases that you are considering and the best steps that you can take to grow your portfolio. You can give some instructions and provide your opinion, but they will take over most of the work for your investment for you. If you have no idea what you are doing and you would like someone to hold your hand, the full-service broker is a good option for you.

Another option for brokers is to work with what is known as a discount broker. These brokers will cost you less than a full-service broker, but remember that it also means you will receive fewer services from them. You must put in more time and effort to get your investments done. However, they will help you to save some money and can really assist you to get some of the advice that you need in the investment world.

Consider a reinvestment plan

You can, while you are working on which stocks to go with, decide to work with one individual company. When you work with this company, you can take the profits that you earn through dividends, and then use that money to purchase more stocks through the same company. As you are first getting started, you will find that you may not be able to invest much, which will limit how many stocks you are able to purchase. When you take that money and reinvest it to get more stocks, rather than taking and personally using the money for your own reasons, can help you to get more profit in the future because you will own more stocks. Over time, your money will start to grow more, and it can help to reduce your risk of investing all at the same time.

Direct investing plans

Since you are a new investor, you will be able to choose whether you would like to work with a direct investment plan. With this kind of investment, you would not have to use a broker to make your purchases, which will save you some fees that you would spend on that person. For this one, you will choose to work directly with the individual company that you want to invest in. You will not go through the stock exchange, but rather, you will go through the company directly to purchase your stocks. There will be a few extra fees that will come with using this option, but they are smaller than what you will find with a broker, so it is a good way to save some money.

This one can be considered similar to the last option, but you will still be able to keep the dividends when you are done, rather than reinvesting those profits. You could choose to use that money to purchase more stocks, but it is not necessary to be considered a direct investment plan. You may want to work with this option if you feel like working with only one company and you don't think that working with a broker is necessary.

All of these options will help you to get your foot in the door of the stock market so that you can start to invest and earn a profit. Remember that in the beginning, you will probably only make a little bit of money, and you may even need to bring in a broker to do the work for you if you are confused, but the point is that you get started and find the option that works the best for you. Take a look through some of the options above and find the one that is sure to fit your style and give you the profits that you want.

Chapter 4

What Options Do I Have For Stock Market Investing?

There are quite a few options that you will be able to choose when you are ready to invest in the stock market. You will need to learn how to narrow down the niche and the industry that you want to work in to make things a little bit easier. While it is important to diversify your portfolio at some point, it is best for a new investor to keep things small.

The strategy that you choose to help you start investing will depend on a number of factors. Sometimes it depends on the money that you have to start with and how much you want to make. Sometimes it depends on the amount of risk involved or the research that you have done on the topic. But even when you have a good plan with lots of research, there are reasons why you should be skeptical and take your time with everything. In this chapter, we will talk about some of the options and even some of the niches that you can choose to help you invest in the right stocks for you.

Dividend Stocks

The first strategy that you can choose is to work with dividend stocks, and it works the best if you would like to pick out a long-term investment. Dividend stocks may not make you rich overnight, but it will help you to earn a lot of money consistently over many years. When going with dividend stocks, you want to make sure that you are picking stocks from companies that are doing well now and are projected to do well in the future. There are quite a few companies who will work out well for this, and if you pick the right one, you will be able to enjoy a percentage of the profits from that company each quarter for as long as you hold the stocks.

Now, it is important to realize that not all stocks that are available on the exchange will work with dividends. This means that you need to check with each company before deciding to use them for this process. Screening companies is a good idea as well because this will help you to figure out which companies will actually give you a dividend each quarter (if the company doesn't make a profit, they are not able to provide their shareholders with any dividends). Each company that trades on the stock exchange will need to put out financial statements. Make sure to utilize these to help you make good decisions.

As you go through your research, you should be able to come up with a list of companies that pay their shareholders a decent dividend. But you do not want to start out with too many companies, so it is now time to narrow the list down a little bit to find those that meet all your criteria. Some of the things that you should look into with each company that you are interested in will include:

- Look to see if the company has had a steady history of paying out their dividends. It is not a good thing if there is a lot of missed dividend payments because this could show that there are some major issues with the company. It is best to go through their history as far as possible to see how consistent the dividend payments are.

- The next thing to look for is how high the return on equity is for this company. To make sure that you are picking out a good company, you need to look over the past five years and see a return on equity of at least fifteen percent if not higher.
- Each share that you are considering needs to have rising earnings and sales over time. If the shares are going down, then you know that you will lose money if you go with this stock.
- The dividends that are provided to the shareholders need to grow as well. This means that you will earn more money over time, instead of getting the exact same amount every year. A good company will see a growth in their dividends of at least five percent over ten years.

Take a look at the list of companies that you are interested in and check to see if they meet some of the requirements above. If they do, then they are a great option to go with, and you should consider investing your money in them.

Foreign stock investing

Another option that you can choose to go with is the foreign stock investing. This is an option that most beginners do not stick with because it is hard to follow what is going on in a foreign market. This means that if you want to go into this type of market, you need to do some extra research and pay special attention to what is going on in other countries. If you do this process correctly, there are a lot of companies overseas that are promising and can bring in more money than you can get in your own country. However, it is important to realize that some risks come with working with foreign stock investing.

There are actually a few benefits that you can enjoy when it comes to investing in foreign stocks. Some of the benefits that you will enjoy with these stock options include:

- The stocks that are available in foreign markets will provide you with some new investment opportunities. Based on your goals for investing, it sometimes is a little hard to find a company that you want to invest in,

especially if you limit yourself to your own country. You may find that it is easier to find the right investments when you look in other markets.
- Foreign stocks can be a good option for those who are looking for new ways to diversify their portfolios. This can help you to spread out some of your risks, so consider investing your money into a variety of companies, even if you are looking at foreign markets.

While these benefits are really tempting for a beginner who wants to find lucrative companies to invest in, it is important to remember that working in a foreign market actually provides a much higher risk than working in the stock exchange in your market. Even if the company looks like a good and safe investment, it is important to take into account the exchange rate. Depending on which market you go into and the amount of dividend that you expect to make, the cost of exchanging the currency over to USD may take all your profits, which makes the risk of investing in these markets higher than before.

The market conditions are often going to be very

different in another country compared to what is going on in your country. For example, the United States may be seeing an upturn in their economy while other countries deal with economies that are shaky. It does not matter what is going on in your home country; what matters is what is going on in whatever country you would like to invest in. This can be good news if the economy in your home country is doing poorly, but it is still something to be aware of.

While there is a lot of potential to make a high profit when you decide to invest in a foreign market, it is very risky, and that is why a lot of beginners choose to not go with this option at all. It may be a good idea to find a good broker and get some help if you decide to go with this as your investment option.

Penny stocks

Penny stocks are an option for investing that some people like to work with, but you have to realize that these are really risky. Beginners like these stocks because they are less expensive than some of the bigger names that are on the stock exchange. If you do not have a lot of money to get started with for this investment, the penny stocks can be a good option for you to go with because you may be better able to afford them.

It is important to realize that not all the companies on the penny stock exchange are reputable. These companies do not need to disclose financial information, and they do not need to meet the same requirements thatcompanies on the stock exchange need to. While there are some companies who will sell shares on this exchange to help them out while they are trying to meet the requirements of the stock exchange (and these are often really good companies to consider because their prices will go up), there are also a lot of failing companies that are working as penny stocks.

This can make it hard to know who you should work with. These penny stocks are really risky, and it is not always the best idea for a beginner to get into this market. Sometimes the value of the stock is hard to figure out, and even a little bit of negative movement can cause a big impact on your investment. Many times these companies are able to hide information from you, and you can lose out your whole investment in no time. These stocks are really volatile as well, which makes it harder to watch the market and make good decisions.

If you are a beginner and you are interested in checking out penny stocks and learning how they work, then you need to be careful and fully aware of all the risks that come with it. Some of the guidelines that you can consider following when you want to get into penny stocks and still see a return on your investment include:

- Pay attention to some of the warnings that you see. There are some regulators on this market, and if they are sending out some warnings about a particular company, it is worth your time to pay attention.
- Don't always believe what you see. These companies are not held up to the same standards as companies on the stock exchange are. Do your own research and learn as much about the company as possible.
- Learn some more about how penny stocks work. We talked briefly about them, but it is so important to take a look at these stocks and

learn more about them before you enter the market.

- Some companies will offer penny stocks, but they are not going to provide you with a lot of information. The less information that is present in a company, the bigger the risk there is to invest in them. Double check that a company is as honest as possible with their information, especially financial information, before you decide to invest.

These are some of the main options that you can work with when you are ready to invest your money in the stock market. Make sure to look through each category and decide which one is the best for your needs.

Chapter 5

Picking Out Your Investment Strategy

Now that we have spent some time looking at all the different options that you have available when picking out a stock, it is time to pick out the strategy that you want to use when it is time to invest in the stock market. There are various strategies that you can work with, and all of them can help you to earn money. The biggest issue with the investment strategy is that you need to fully understand how it works. If you don't understand the strategy or you keep mixing it up with other ones, you will not see success.

So, the first thing that we need to do here is to learn a bit more about the different investment strategies that you can choose from. There are a lot of options, but you must understand how they work if you want any hope for success. Let's take a look at some of the most popular investment strategies and how they should work.

Working with the fundamental analysis

The first investment strategy that we will look at is called a fundamental analysis. This is an easy option to work with, but it does take some time, and you will need to bring out some of your research skills. The goal of working with this kind of analysis is that you want to look at the company that you want to invest in and then figure out what the intrinsic value of that company is. This means that you want to figure out how much the stock of that company is worth when compared to the current value that the company has on the stock exchange.

If the intrinsic value of that company is already higher than what the company is currently trading for, it is a good idea to make a purchase of that stock. When this happens, it means that there is a high likelihood that the stock will go up in price in the near future and you will make money if you enter into the trade at the right time.

Next on the list to figure out is which method you would like to use to help you figure out the intrinsic value of our chosen company. There may be some similarities between these methods, but it is important to pick one. First, you could start out by taking a look at the sum of the discounted cash flows for that company. What this means is that the company will be worth all its future profits when you add them together. Then you can take these projected future profits and discount them so that you can account for what is known as time value, or the force that says that $1 today will be worthless when you get to the future because of inflation.

The idea of the intrinsic value of the company being equal to the future profit will help you to understand how a company can provide more value to its owners. Think about owning your own business and how its worth will include all the money that you can take in as profit when you get to the end of the year. This is only going to be possible if you make a profit after you pay your debts, salaries, suppliers, and other bills first and then have some money left over. This is what you want to find when you look at a company to invest in.

So, where are you going to find some of these numbers? You should be able to find these directly from the company and their financial reports. These reports are required before the company is able to join the stock exchange, which makes it easy for you to take a look through them. You should also take some time to dig deeper and look at the news about a particular company to figure out what numbers are being announced to the public. When you are able to bring all of this information together, it is much easier to help you go through this analysis and pick out the companies that are best for you.

Value investing

Another option or strategy that you can go with when you are ready to invest in the stock market is called value investing. This is actually a really popular strategy that you can try out because it is so successful. When you work with value investing, you will go with a company that has really strong fundamentals, such as strong book value, cash flow, dividends, and earnings. You will then take all that information and compare it to what the stocks are selling for on the market.

When you are a value investor, you will need to look for companies which are undervalued on the market, no matter what the reason, compared to their fundamentals. When a company is undervalued, it means that you are able to purchase their stocks for a great price. As long as the fundamentals of that company are strong, it is very likely that the price of those stocks will increase to their market value, and sometimes higher, once everyone else catches on. You can make a lot of good money with this option as long as you pick a company that fits the bill and you get on it quickly.

Now, it is important to realize that there is a difference between a junk stock and one that is undervalued. If you go with the junk stocks just because they are lower in price, you will end up in some trouble. When you are looking through the market, there are always some companies who will have lower-priced stocks. This is not because those companies are undervalued, but because these companies are just not worth all that much. These companies could have some other issues with them, such as high debt to profit ratio, bad management, or some other reason that they are not worth much.

When you are looking at value stocks, you are looking

at companies that actually have good dividends, low debt, and a strong earning potential. Often there is something in the market that is working against them, and so the value of the stock is discounted temporarily. If this is true about the company, then it is likely that their value will go up in no time.

Some beginners do not like to work with value investing. They may feel that most stocks will be at the price where they should be and that it does not matter what the fundamentals are. They may figure that if a stock is supposed to be ranked at a higher price, then it would be at that higher price. There are some investors, on the other hand, who like this method because it helps them to find some good stock investments without having to jump in too late in the game.

CAN SLIM

You can also try using a strategy that goes under the acronym of CAN SLIM. This one will take on a few extra steps to help you see success, but it may be just what a beginner needs to ensure that they are doing the proper research before picking out a new stock to invest in. Let's take a look at what all of these parts mean and how they can help you to pick out a good stock to invest in.

C = Current earnings

With this part, you need to look at the company and see how much they are earning now in the present. You can look at the most recent quarter of the company and then see how it compares to what was made in that same quarter the year before. If this is a solid company, then you should notice that the profits went up from one year to the next. If the profits went down, the company could be experiencing some issues that you want to avoid. It is a good idea to see a growth of twenty percent or more to ensure that you have less risk in the investment.

A = Annual earnings

Now, we will take a look at how much earnings for the company have grown over the past year. You should not just look over one year, though. It is best to look through at least the past five years, if not more, of that company. When you are looking through these five years, you should see that each year has at least a little bit of growth. It is ideal if the growth over the full five years is about twenty-five percent if not more.

N = New

You can also take a look at the company and then find out if some new changes occurred within the company. There are a lot of changes that a business can go through - some will harm the company, and others are good for the company. If you see that some of the harmful changes are being implemented, it is best to leave that organization behind. But if there are some changes in a product being released or within management, it could increase the value of the corporation in the near future.

S = supply and demand

For this criteria, you must take a look at how the supply and the demand of that company is doing. This helps you to know how much the price of the stock is likely to go up in the future. If all things are considered equal in the market, it is easier for some of the smaller firms, who will have fewer shares, to show more gains compared to the bigger ones. The reason for this is because the larger companies will need to deal with a higher demand than some smaller companies just to get it to show up as gains at all.

L = Leader

Here we will take a look at the leaders and the laggards in the market and see how these are able to change your decisions. No matter which industry you will work in, there will be some companies who are considered the leaders. These are the ones that will provide the best dividends to their shareholders. Conversely, there are a few companies who will be lagging behind in the industry, and they are not able to provide a good return on investment to their shareholders. Make sure that you are picking out a company that will be one of the leaders if you would like to make the most money possible.

I = Institutional Sponsorship

The reason that you want to work with institutional sponsorship is because you will be able to see that the company is popular. If you are looking for a company and it doesn't have this kind of sponsorship at all, this means that many money managers have decided not to use this company and there is usually a big red flag reason why they didn't. It is best to pick out a company that has a minimum of three of these institutional owners.

You do need to be watchful if a company has too many of these institutions involved in the process. There is such a thing as a company being owned too much by institutions, and when this happens, it means it is too late for you to get into this company. If you do get into the company, you will probably lose out when those institutions decide to sell the company off. You want a few money managers to be involved, but not too many that it all becomes too congested.

M = Market direction

And the final thing that you will take a look at is the market direction. Any time that you wish to look at a new stock, it is important to look through the market conditions and figure out whether you are dealing with a bear or a bull market. If you do not understand where the market is heading, this will cause a big amount of risk to your gains, and it will be much easier to make some bad decisions on your investment.

Income investing

Another option that you can choose when you are picking out an investment strategy is known as income investing. With income investing, you need to look over the company and then decide whether they are able to provide you with a fairly steady stream of income. This is an easier method, and many beginners like to work with it. When you think about the investment as a way to make a steady income, instead of a way to make money quickly, it is easier to pick out less risky options. There are a variety of options that you would be able to work with for this, such as bonds and fixed income security. There are a number of stocks that can also do this as long as you pick the right one.

To make the income investment work for you, you must be careful that you pick out stocks that will provide a dividend that will be around for a long time. Remember that the average yield for most dividend stocks will be somewhere around three percent. But if you are looking to use this dividend as a way to make an income, then you need to go with a stock that can provide you with a profit of six percent, if not higher, or you are wasting your time.

Of course, in addition to looking through the market and picking out the stocks that will provide you with a steady income stream, you also need to read through the policies that the company releases about the dividends. This can be important because some companies will not keep handing out the dividends in the future. You can also look through this information to see whether the company added some more dividends as this will affect your profits as well. For example, if you see that the company increased their dividend plans by quite a bit over the last year, this is usually an overly optimistic position, and it is best to go with another company to protect your investment.

Income investing is a long-term solution. This is not a method that you will join and then sell out quickly when the market turns on you. The whole point is to provide you with an income each quarter that you are able to use just like any other income that you bring in. The trick here is that you need to be able to find the companies who will be able to provide you with this kind of income.

Dogs of the Dow

Some beginner investors like to work with the strategy that is known as Dogs of the Dow. This is a simple approach that is meant to help you make your money over the long-term. If you are looking to chase the market around and hope to make money quickly, this is not going to be the right option for you. For this strategy, you will look at the 30 companies that have been listed in the DIJA or the Dow Jones Industrial Average. From here, you will pick out ten investments that are performing really well. After you have finished with that first year, you will take a look at the list again, and pick the ten that are doing well for the second year. This does require some readjusting to your portfolio but helps you to pick out companies that are always doing well.

Every few years or so, you may need to make some adjustments and get rid of some of the stocks that you own. You will replace them with new stocks that are now in the top of the DIJA to help you do well. This is hard to keep up with sometimes, but going off that list will make things so much easier.

With this strategy, just like when you pick out any of the other strategies that are on this list, Dogs of the Dow is not necessarily foolproof, and there are times when it is not going to provide you with the return on investment that you would like. Generally, though, it is a good way to find companies that are doing well and can provide you with a good return on investment. If you are a beginner and don't know how to work in the market, or you are worried about finding time to research the right companies to invest in, then this is the right option for you.

The reason that a lot of beginners choose to go with Dogs of the Dow is that
it is really simple to understand. You will be able to save a lot of time by not having to look through all those charts, and yet you will still be able to see some good results with your investment. All that you need to do is set aside some time when a new year starts and look at this list. Then you go through and make the changes that are necessary to your portfolio so

that everything matches up the right way. There are a few times that you will need to make changes to the stocks you are holding, but many of them will stay the same from year to year, so the work on this strategy is minimal.

There are many strategies that you are able to choose from when it comes to working in the stock market, and we have only brought up a few of the ones that you may be interested in. All of them can be successful as long as you follow them correctly. Pick out the one that is the most comfortable for you and you will start to make a good return on investment in no time.

Chapter 6

Different Styles That Expert Traders Use for Stock Trading

It is also possible to get into the stock market and do what is known as stock trading. Stock trading is a little bit different because you are not focusing on the long-term with this option. Instead, you are focusing on how to make a profit more quickly in the stock market. You will try to purchase stocks when they are low, such as when the company is undervalued or right before the value of the company is expected to go up, and then you will sell them in the future for a profit. This can work well if you know how to read the market and you are willing to take the risk. Sometimes you will only hold onto your position for a day or less and other times you may hold this position for a few months, but it is never meant to be a long-term investment type, and you likely will not hold onto the stocks long enough to earn any dividends.

If you want to go with the option of stock trading, then it is imperative that you learn how to read the market and that you are willing to move fast. You may be able to purchase a stock at a discount or a very low price, and then you must sell it when that stock price goes up. The hardest part is to figure out when a stock is low because it is discounted or the market is low, or when a stock is low because the company is not worth much. If you pick a stock from one of the latter, then the price will never go up, and you will not make a profit.

If you are interested in giving stock trading a try, there are a few options that you can look into to get the most out of your money. As you learn how to use these strategies and get into the market for some time, you will be able to bring your own personal style into the mix as well. Let's take a look at some of these styles and see how they can help you become successful with stock trading.

Position trading

Some of the styles that you can do with stock trading will require you to get in and out of the market within a few days if not sooner. This can be a bit intense for a lot of beginners to the stock market, and you may not want to try that until you get more comfortable. Position trading is a good option if you would like to have some room when it comes to the trading period between purchasing and selling your stock. Many of these trades can last for a few months, and some for even longer.

The benefit of working with position trading is that you will be able to hold onto the stock for a little bit longer so you can watch the trends in the market before selling. If things go south, you will have more time to hold onto the stock and wait it out until the market goes up. There are a lot of sudden changes that can occur with a stock from day to day, even with a steadier stock, and this method will give you some room to breathe.

Of course, this one is more similar to stock market investing than some of the others because you are holding onto the stock for a longer period of time. However, you can choose to make it more of a short-term trade. Instead of holding onto the stocks for years, you may only hold onto the stock for a few weeks. As a position trader, it will become your job to look at weekly as well as monthly charts to help you make some good trading decisions. You will not really need to spend your time looking at short-term price changes with this strategy.

Day trading

Some traders want to work on a short-term investment inside the stock market. Day trading can be the answer to that because it is a fast-paced option that can be hard to keep up with. If you are not willing to constantly watch the market or you are not willing to take some risks, then day trading is not the option for you. As a day trader, it will be your job to purchase a stock sometime during the day, usually in the morning, and then you will need to sell that stock before the market closes on that same day. You are not allowed to keep your stocks longer than this so you will need to sell, regardless of whether you end up with a winning or losing position.

Day traders look at the market differently than the position trader will. They do not care how the stock will do over the long-term because they do not plan to hold that stock for more than a few hours. However, they are really interested in how the stock has been doing over the past few days. When they are able to see a good trend, they will be better able to make some predictions about what will happen with their stocks. This helps them to make some good purchasing decisions.

Day trading is not going to yield you a lot of money off each trade. No stock sees huge increases in prices in just a few hours. But if you do a lot of little trades throughout the week, you will be able to make a good deal of profits from this trading method.

Swing trading

Swing trading is another option that you can choose to go with when you want to get into stock trading. With this trading style, you will purchase the stocks that you want to use, hold onto them for up to two weeks, and then sell them at a higher price. This is similar to day trading, but you will get up to a few weeks rather than just a few hours.

A swing trader will look at a stock and try to

determine if that stock value will go up in the next few weeks. Perhaps they have been doing some research, and they see that a big announcement is about to come out concerning a company. That company's stocks may be pretty low at that moment, but because of a new expansion or a new product launch, the price of the stock may be expected to go up. The swing trader would purchase the stock when the price is low, hold onto it for a few weeks, and then sell to make a profit.

The fundamentals of a company are not going to matter as much with swing trading because you are not going to hold your position for all that long. The swing trader is just looking for companies that are likely to see an increase in the price and value of their stocks sometime in the near future. It doesn't really matter to them who runs the company or how much they pay out in dividends because the swing trader is not planning on being in the market that long.

Scalp trading

Some traders will choose to work in what is known as scalp trading. This can be considered similar to day trading, but you will be much busier with this option. Your goal as a scalp trader is to be constantly purchasing and selling your stocks non-stop throughout the day. The main agenda for the scalp trader is to focus on the day to day changes of the stock market because this will help them determine when to make a purchase and when to sell.

The scalper has the goal of purchasing a stock at a low price, and then they will sell it as soon as the price goes up. Since the market is constantly going up and down, this is possible as long as you are able to pay close attention to what is going on in the market. You often will only make a small amount on each sale, but if you do hundreds of these during the same day, it can quickly add up.

Picking your trading style

Above, you learned about some of the best trading styles that you can use if you would like to work with stock trading. Now that you have learned about them a little bit, it is time to pick out the one that you would like to use. But how are you going to make this kind of decision if you have never traded in the stock market?

Some of the questions that you should ask yourself when picking out a new trading style include:

- How big is my account?
- How much risk am I willing to take to make a profit?
- What is my trading personality?
- Do I have any experience with trading or am I just getting started and need to work on something easier?
- How much time will I be able to devote to my trades? Position trading just needs to be checked on occasion while scalping and day trading will require you to spend a lot of time watching the market.

For most investors, the amount of risk that they are willing to take and the amount of time that they have available for trading will determine which trading style they choose to go with. It is not possible for everyone to give up all their time, at least in the beginning, to the trading method, but that is what options like scalping will require. Others may not be willing to take on that much risk just to get a little bit of profit. It is all going to depend on what you would like to get out of this investment and your own trading personality.

In the beginning, just pick out one style that you are willing to work with. In time, as you earn more money and get more experience with the stock market, you can start diversifying your portfolio a bit more and can add in more of these styles to the mix. This will help you to make a lot more money in the long-term, but it is best to start out slow as a beginner.

Chapter 7

Rules That Help to Reduce Your Risks When Investing in the Stock Market

As a beginner in the stock market, it is important that you learn some of the best ways to reduce your risk. The stock market can be a good way to make money, but many beginners will fall prey to some of the mistakes that make this a really big risk. There is enough risk in the investment on its own, so you need to find ways to reduce your risks to make as much money as possible. Some of the steps that you can take to ensure that you are getting the most out of your investment include:

Do not follow the crowd

When you decide to get into stock market investing, you must learn how to make decisions on your own. It is tempting to always listen to your broker or to listen to the friend who has been on the market for a long time. While it is just fine for you to take the advice of others when you are getting started, you must remember that this is your investment. No one else has money on the line when you pick a certain stock or go with a certain strategy - only you do.

What this means is that you can still ask for advice and suggestions from other people. Talking to your broker and some friends who may know the market a little bit better is fine. However, take everything with a grain of salt. You will run into troubles if you hear what someone else says and then jump right in without even thinking about the investment. Always do your own research and use your own judgment to figure out which investments are the best for you.

Pick out a strategy and always stick with it

As you should know by now, there are a lot of different strategies that you can work with when it is time to invest in the stock market. All of these strategies have the potential of making you money, but you need to make sure that you fully understand the strategy that you are working with. If you are not using the method in the proper way, you will not be able to make money.

You also need to make sure that when you pick a strategy, you are sticking with that strategy the whole time. It is easy for a beginner to see a new approach that they think is good, but then try to switch right in the middle of a trade because it is not going the way that they want. This is dangerous. You are never going to succeed when you are splitting up two strategies. There are times, no matter which strategy that you pick, where you are not going to make money, and that is okay. You should just leave the market and call it good, rather than losing more money because you tried to switch your game plan.

You may be tempted to switch out your strategy because you do not fully understand how to manage itor because you start losing money. However, the second that you try to switch during a trade, the harder it will be to make money and keep your investment safe. You can always switch out strategies when the trade is done if you do not like using the one you picked, but stick it out until the trade is done.

Forget about the timing

Timing the market is never a good idea. There are a lot of beginners who will try to figure out how to time the stock market, but they often end up losing a lot of money rather than earning anything. Experts in all industries agree that it is pretty much impossible to find the exact tops and exact bottoms of a stock, and if you happen to reach them, it was because you are lucky, not because of good planning.

The issue here is that you can't predict how other people will react to a market. You can make some good guesses, but it is impossible to tell for certain when people will start selling or buying a particular stock. If you are trying to buy at the exact lowest point and then sell at the exact highest point, you will miss out on a lot of great opportunities. What you need to focus on instead is finding when the stock is at a good discount for your purchase and then selling the stock when it gets above its market value. This may not give you maximum profit, but you will earn a profit, and it helps you to avoid staying in the market too long.

Some financial advisors insist that timing the market

is the only way that you can make a good profit in the stock market. The issue with this is that this strategy is often going to backfire on you. Additionaly, while it affects you quite a bit, it will have no effect on the advisor. If you spend too much of your time trying to outsmart the market, you will be the one who loses.

Only invest what you can afford

When you see a good investment opportunity, it is tempting to jump in and use all the money that you have. You may go out and use all your savings and some of the money from your paychecks this month in the hopes that it will turn out well and you will become rich. But what happens if the investment doesn't go the way that you plan? Now you have nothing, and you may not even be able to pay your bills the next month.

One of the best practices that you can do when you get started with stock investing is that you only invest the money that you would be comfortable with losing. No one wants to lose money on an investment, but it is something that can happen. If you go into the market assuming that you will never lose, you are setting yourself up for a lot of trouble. Perhaps you should consider setting up a savings account ahead of time and putting some money in to help you with your investments without worrying that you are investing too much. No matter which method you choose to go with, make sure that you only add in the amount of money to the investment that wouldn't be disastrous if you end up losing.

Keep your expectations realistic

There are a lot of beginners who will join the stock market and hope that they are able to make a lot of money. They may hear that it is possible to lose money in this market, but they figure that they can outsmart the market and that they will not end up losing all that much in the process. However, this is a bad way to enter the market. Even seasoned stock market investors who have been doing this for years will still lose money. There are many times when the market does something that you do not expect, and you can lose money no matter how much you plan.

In addition, going into the market and thinking you will earn money overnight is a bad idea. Some investments could potentially make you rich, but these are really risky. It is unlikely that you will actually succeed because the risk is so high, and you will most likely lose more money than you can afford to lose.

Going into the stock market is risky enough. Do not make it worse by going into the market with expectations that are not all that realistic. Understand that you can make some money in this investment, but it will often take some time to see that success. You must also understand that there are some times, no matter how hard you plan ahead, when you will end up losing money in the process.

Keep the emotions out of the game

You also need to make sure that you are able to keep emotions out of the game. As soon as those emotions come into play, you will start losing money. These emotions will often lead you to make poor decisions, and you are more likely to lose out on your investment.

This is why having a good strategy in place will make

all the difference when it comes to making money with the stock market. This strategy will set up all the rules that you need to follow. It will tell you when to enter the market when you should leave the market, and all the steps in between. It basically outlines what you need to do, taking most of the decisions out of the game and allowing you to keep your emotions away as well.

One thing that you must learn to avoid at all costs is revenge trading. This starts when you end up losing some money on one trade because you made bad decisions or the market did not react the way that you wanted. Instead of just taking the loss and learning from it, you decide that you need to start making that money back right away. You go into risky investment options in the hopes of earning that money back quickly. Often investors who choose to go with revenge trading will not think through their decisions. The only thinking that they do is that they want to earn the money back. They will pick bad investments and not listen to the advice of others along the way. Because of this, they often lose a ton more money than they would have if they just learned from the mistake and moved on.

If you are someone who is really emotional or can let their decisions be affected by what is going on around them, or if you are worried about losing money in the process of trading, then investing in the stock market may not be the right choice. There are times when the market will not behave the way that you want, and there isn't much you can do about it. For these kinds of people, there are a lot of other investments, including ones that are less risky, that can help you earn good money as well.

Set your stop points

Another thing that you can consider doing is to set up some stop points. These are basically the points when you will exit the market, both when you are making profits and when you are losing. These can help to minimize your risks because you will make the decisions about these stop points before you enter the market and money is at stake. If you forget to do these, it can sometimes be hard to get out of the market at the right time, no matter how much logic you use.

The first stop point that you need to set is the one

where you will exit the market when you are losing money. While you never want to think about losing money, it is much better to do this before you put any money in. This stop point should be at a place where you would still be comfortable with losing that money if things go wrong. Then, as soon as the market reaches that point, you will exit the market, no matter what may happen later on.

Some beginners find that it is tempting to stay in the market, even when they are losing money. They figure that the market will return and that they will be able to recoup their losses if they just stay in. This rarely ever works, and if you keep in the market, you are likely to keep losing money. With this stop point, you can keep your losses to a minimum and re-enter the market later on if you decide to.

You should also consider adding in a stop point to exit when you have made enough profits. Yes, it would be nice to plan for unlimited profits, but this is not going to happen, no matter which industry you choose to invest in. Adding this stop point in will ensure that you get some profit. Without it, you may be tempted to stay in the market too long, and when the market turns, you may end up losing all that profit and more.

It is best to set up these stop points ahead of time for each trade before you invest any money into the market. This will ensure that you are making logical decisions, long before the emotions can come into play, and you will be surprised at what a difference it can make in the amount of profit that you enjoy with this investment.

As a beginner in the stock market, there are a lot of things that you need to consider. You have to understand how the market works, which stocks to pick, when to get into and out of the market, and so much more. However, if you follow the tips and tricks in this guidebook and stick to the rules in this chapter, you will see the amazing results that you want.

Conclusion

Thank you for making it through to the end of this book! Let's hope it was informative and able to provide you with all of the tools you need to achieve your goals - whatever they may be.

The next step is to take a look at which investment strategy you would like to use when it comes to working with stock market investing. There are many different investment opportunities that you can go with, but the stock market provides the most variety, and the most fun, when it comes to putting your money to work for you.

Finally, if you found this book useful in any way, a review on Amazon is always appreciated!

Options Trading

The Complete Guide to Trading Options

(Secret Hints and Tips Only the Professionals Know)

©Copyright 2018 by - All rights reserved.

The following eBook is reproduced below with the goal of providing information that is as accurate and reliable as possible. Regardless, purchasing this eBook can be seen as consent to the fact that both the publisher and the author of this book are in no way experts on the topics discussed within and that any recommendations or suggestions that are made herein are for entertainment purposes only. Professionals should be consulted as needed prior to undertaking any of the action endorsed herein.

This declaration is deemed fair and valid by both the American Bar Association and the Committee of Publishers Association and is legally binding throughout the United States.

Furthermore, the transmission, duplication or reproduction of any of the following work including specific information will be considered an illegal act irrespective of whether it is done electronically or in print. This extends to creating a secondary or tertiary copy of the work or a recorded copy and is only allowed with an express written consent from the Publisher. All additional rights reserved.

The information in the following pages is broadly considered to be a truthful and accurate account of facts and, as such, any inattention, use or misuse of the information in question by the reader will render any resulting actions solely under their purview. There are no scenarios in which the publisher or the original author of this work can be in any fashion deemed liable for any hardship or damages that may befall them after undertaking information described herein.

Additionally, the information in the following pages is intended only for informational purposes and should thus be thought of as universal. As befitting its nature, it is presented without assurance regarding its prolonged validity or interim quality. Trademarks that are mentioned are done without written consent and can in no way be considered an endorsement from the trademark holder.

Introduction

Congratulations on downloading this book and thank you for doing so.

In this world, money matters—a lot. Don't let anyone advise you otherwise. The people who are preaching otherwise either have a lot of it or are incapable of earning it. This is the hard reality of this world. People go on saying that money can't buy you everything. However, they forget to mention that you can't buy the rest of the things that money can if you don't have enough of it. You can preach about the disadvantages of money ONLY when you have a lot of it.

Therefore, earning money is important. The fact that you're reading this book right now suggests that you already realize its importance. You want to earn more of it and earn it fast. Options trading is a good and LEGITIMATE way to earn money. The legitimate part is important as there are also other methods that might put you in the bad books of law enforcement, and you must avoid those.

Now we come to the option at hand, and that is **Options Trading**. First of all, there is no magic trick. There is no free lunch either, and, as a full disclosure, there are risks involved. If you work in haste, do not pay attention to the market indicators, and take serious risks, then you can lose your money in options trading. However, you can still lose money even if you take all the precautions in everything else in life. Options trading runs on the market and market forces act on it. This means that, sometimes, things can go wrong even if you are extra careful. But that is a rare scenario. You must never put all your eggs in the same basket, and that's a very important rule. If you keep that in mind, then only a situation like a complete market crash can cause you a catastrophic loss.

One important aspect of options trading is that it is a speculative trade. People will try to discourage you by saying that things can go wrong all the way for you. Let that not deter you in any way. If options trading is a speculative game, then the whole stock exchange is running on speculations. Every day, people invest in various commodities, expecting them to rise or fall and to make money from them. The options trading field is no different. On the contrary, it keeps your risks low because your investment is small. When you enter into an options trade, you know the highest amount of money you can lose, and that is the invested capital. In options trading, this capital is small as compared to the investment required in real stock. This makes it comparatively safe or less risky.

You cannot expect to make it big in the stock market with small capital. Options trading gives you a chance to enter the market even with a small amount and gain profit as others with big money do.

This book will help you in understanding the basic concepts of options trading. It will show you ways people can make money in the options trade as well as things that can cause losses. It will give you tips on understanding the risks and avoiding temptations. It will explain that, although the option trade runs on speculation, it is not a complete gamble. There are several calculations going on all the time. The psychology of the option buyer and the option seller will also be explained so that you know how things actually work.

This is not a very cordial world. The competition is

cutthroat and everyone wants to excel even at the cost of others. Options trading gives you a chance to earn money in a fair way. You can start with a modest sum and earn money by keeping a track of the market. You will need patience and the ability to learn from your mistakes to excel in the market. If you are ready for the challenge, then the market is open for you with its arms outstretched and welcoming. This will be your introduction to the concepts of options trading.

There are plenty of books on this subject on the market, thanks again for choosing this one! Every effort was made to ensure it contains as much useful information as possible. Please enjoy!

Chapter 1

Understanding the Options Trade

Let us understand the functioning of an options trade. We'll take the analogy of Tom and Jerry.

Tom owns a cheese manufacturing unit. It has a fine production as well as steady clients. However, Tom is not content with it. He has bigger dreams.

One day, Jerry comes to Tom and asks him to sell the cheese production unit to him. He proposes a good market rate of $100K for the plant. Tom feels the offer to be good.

Jerry asks Tom for the rights to buy the cheese plant by the last Friday of the following month. He deposits a security amount of 2%. Tom is happy. He gets $2000 right away, while he also has the plant for the time being. But now he cannot sell the plant to anyone else until the last Friday of the next month.

Jerry is happy because now he has the right to buy the

plant by the given date at a set price. But he doesn't have an obligation to do so.

This means that Jerry can buy the plant within that period at a set price of $100K irrespective of the rate of the property in that area. Even if the rates were to increase, his purchase would remain good and secure. If the prices in the area go down, the cheese unit starts performing badly or loses its customers, or he loses his interest in the plant, he can simply forget the deal. He can choose not to buy. In that case, he would also have to forget his initial security deposit of $2000.

In the event of a significant change in the prices of the commodity, Jerry can exercise his discretion to buy or sell the commodity at a higher or lower cost and make a profit, but his purchase price would remain fixed. Tom cannot ask a higher price from him due to the inflation in the market.

However, the security deposit is the amount that goes to Tom in lieu of his assurance to sell the commodity to Jerry by a set date for a set price.

Tom has an obligation, and not a choice, to sell the

commodity to Jerry at that price. Tom can enjoy the security deposit in the meantime.

If Jerry doesn't buy that commodity, the security deposit will be forfeited by Tom.

Definition:

An options trade is a contract that gives you the right, but not an obligation, to buy or sell a commodity before a set date for a set price. There are three very important parts of this trade:

- You must know the commodity you are going to buy or sell.
- You must know the price range of the commodity you are going to buy or sell. The seller is bound to give you the commodity at a predefined rate irrespective of market value at the time of the actual transaction.
- You must make the transaction within the set date. If you fail to buy the product by the agreed date, the contract will expire, and the seller will forfeit your security deposit.

To put it simply:

By paying a token amount (not the full amount), you can register or reserve (pre-book) a product or service to be delivered at a future date at a pre-agreed price.

- *When the day of the expiry of the agreement arrives, you can choose whether or not to avail yourself of that pre-booked product or service.*
- *If you decide not to avail yourself of the product or service, you can forgo your token amount.*
- *If you want to avail yourself of the product or service, you will have to pay the complete price decided at the beginning.*

Now this question pops up: Why wouldn't you want to avail yourself of the product or services?

There can be 2 main reasons:

1. You may lose interest in the product or the service.

2. The price doesn't remain attractive to you anymore. In that case, purchasing the product would become a liability. You can incur further losses. It would be better to leave the product or service and not buy it at all.

An important thing to remember:

An options contract gives you the right to book any product or service at an agreed price, called the ***Strike Price,*** and to be bought by a predefined date, called the ***Expiration Date***. It is your right, but not an obligation, to avail yourself of that product or service. If you choose not to avail yourself of it, you will lose your pre-booking amount. You will have to forgo your token amount, called the ***Premium***. The premium amount is the cost of the privilege or convenience to buy that product or service at a fixed price by a fixed date. It is a non-refundable and non-adjustable amount.

Privilege is a keyword to understand here. You are paying the premium for buying an "option"—an option to buy or not to buy a specific product by a specific date at a price fixed at this moment. The price of the commodity is not included in this premium. It is just the cost of buying the privilege.

The seller of the option has an obligation to provide you the product or service at a predefined rate, by a predefined date. There is a commitment here. It is no longer a choice for the seller of the option contract. This is the reason why the options trade is called the **Options Contract**. The seller is bound to honor the commitment, but you as a buyer are free to exercise your right to buy it or not.

Chapter 2

How The Options Trade Works in Real-Life Scenarios

Now let us understand how an options trade works in a real life market scenario.

First of all, it is a fact that the options trade is speculative in nature. You are practically predicting or assuming that a particular stock will rise in the next few days, months or years. You must have sound reasons for assuming so, as this may cost you.

You have to choose a particular stock prudently based on good reason.

For instance, we take a pharmaceutical stock named ABCL. It is currently trading at $93 per share. You believe that there will be a boom in the pharmaceutical sector, and there are possibilities of this stock going up.

An important thing to note:

Playing on pure hunch can prove to be very risky. You must do your research. Analyze the stock performance, its upper and lower levels, and the way it has been behaving in the past. Find out if there is any positive or negative news about that stock in the market.

Let us consider these scenarios for earning money.

Scenario 1:

You believe that the stock will gain money within next few days. You see that the ABCL stock is currently trading at $93 per share. The call option for the 30th of November is trading at $13 with an expiry date of 90 days. This means that you can sell this stock within 90 days' time if it is trading above $93 and gain profit. The best thing about the options trade is that you don't have to invest the whole $93. You can buy the options at a premium of $13. The options are traded in lots. The lots are of a hundred stocks. This means that to buy the options of ABCL's 100 shares, you'd need $13*100 = $1300. This is much lower than the $9300 to be invested in 100 ABCL stocks.

Pros: You can leverage the power of the market without investing a large amount.

Cons: If the market doesn't move as per your speculations, you can lose all your money invested in that stock.

Scenario 2:

You believe that ABCL's stock is not performing well and that there is a great likelihood that the stock will plummet in the near future. You can buy the put option for the ABCL stock at $13 for the 30th of November expiration date. This means that you can sell the stocks profitably if they go below your speculated price before the said date and make money from them. The lower the stock goes the better profits you will make.

Buying the call and put option works in the same way. The lot size remains fixed and the price of the call or put is predetermined. You agree with a strike price, that is the goal. Whenever the stock goes beyond the strike price, you make money on the trade.

If the stock falls short of the strike price before the

expiration date your options trade will become worthless and you will lose money on it.

The scenarios above are simple concepts to make you understand how the options trade works. You'll also learn that time plays a very important role in the options trade. In the next chapters, the intricacies of the trade and how the premium gets affected by various factors will be explained in detail.

Chapter 3

Understanding the Call Option

As explained earlier, options are contracts between two parties who agree upon the commodity, its price, and the settlement date. All of these factors are non-negotiable. Let us understand this with the help of an analogy.

Mark and John are two traders. John sells copper wires in wholesale, and Mark is interested in purchasing copper wires. Mark goes to John and asks him the price of his copper wires. John tells him that he is selling the copper wires at $2.75/lb. Mark says he wants to buy a bulk quantity as he believes the price of copper wires will increase. He can make a lot of money this way. John agrees to sell him the wires. But there is a catch.

Mark tells John that he expects the price to go up in the next 2 months. He doesn't want his money to be stagnant for so long. He asks John to make an agreement that he will sell the copper wires to him within 2 months at the price of $2.75/lb. John says that he can agree to it if Mark is ready to pay some money right away as a booking amount and the remaining money within 2 months at the time of delivery.

Mark feels the deal to be good, but he is having second thoughts now. He asks what will happen if the market price goes down and if John will agree to sell the copper wires to him at the reduced price. John doesn't agree to this term.

John rebuts that he will not be charging an escalated price if the price of the commodity goes up, so why would he take a lower price if it goes down? It wouldn't be a fair arrangement. He tells Mark that the price is fixed, come what may.

This is not a suitable arrangement for Mark. He wants an arrangement where he can enjoy the tide of rising prices but doesn't have to bear the gloom of the sloppy markets.

But John doesn't agree to this as he also wants to have a favorable deal. He says that he can agree to the deal when he has some assurance.

He gives Mark an option. Mark can buy the agreed quantity of copper wires before a set date at the current fixed price. All three factors will be non-negotiable. This means that Mark can buy 1 mt. of copper wires within 60 days from him at a price of $2.75/lb. However, he will have to pay a premium price of $200 for this deal.

This means that even if the price of copper wires goes beyond $3.75/lb. within 60 days, he will sell them to Mark at the price of $2.75/lb. John can earn the profit from that deal without worrying about an escalated price. However, the premium of $200 paid at the time of buying the options contract will be non-refundable or non-adjustable in the final amount.

If the price of copper wires plummets and takes a deep dive, the price given to Mark will remain the same. He will then have an option to walk away from the deal and forget the premium of $200 paid at the time of the contract. He will have no obligation to honor the contract. Mark's maximum loss will remain restricted to $200, paid as the price of the option.

There are 4 important parts to this deal:

Strike Price: The purchase price of the copper wires is fixed for Mark as $2.75/lb., no matter what price level the item reaches in the stock market. John can't ask for a higher price. This is called the Strike Price.

Expiration Date: The period of the deal is fixed to 60 days from the date of the contract. The call option will have to be exercised prior to this date. It is called the Expiration Date.

Lot Size: The quantity of the deal is fixed at 1 Mt. Anything above that will be at market rate. This quantity is the Lot Size.

Premium: The option price is fixed at $200, which Mark will have to give right away and he will have no claim on it whatsoever. Whether he chooses to buy the copper wires or not, this money is non-refundable and non-adjustable. It is the price of buying the call option (the privilege to buy). This amount is called the Premium.

If the price of copper wires doesn't go up, then Mark can forget the deal and buy the copper wires at market price from anyone.

In that case, his losses would be limited to the premium paid for the call option.

Chapter 4

Understanding the Put Option

Let us extend Mark and John's scenario.

Mark made a profitable deal with the call option of copper wires. The markets had been looking up, and the prices of the copper wires soared. He sold his stock at a good price and made a neat profit. He wants to invest in copper wires again.

This time, Mark feels that the trends are bullish. The demand for copper has been declining and the supply has been good. This will affect its overall price in the market. He knows that buying copper wires can be a risky trade at this time, but he still wants to enter the market and swim with the tide.

He again goes to John and tells him that he wants to sell the copper wires within the next 60 days. He feels that the markets will go down. In that case, he would like to cash in on the opportunity.

John agrees with Mark and makes an offer. He tells Mark that he can buy a sell option of the copper wires at a speculated price of his choice. The current price of copper wires is $2.75/lb. This means he believes it will touch around $2.5/lb. He can buy the sell option of 1 Mt. stock from him at a premium price of $200 to take place within the next 60 days. This means that if the market price of the copper wires goes down to $2.3/lb., he'll be making a profit of $0.2/lb., which is the difference of the amount. The lower the price goes the better profit he will make. John will have an obligation to buy back the stock from Mark at a predetermined price of $2.5/lb. The steeper the fall in the prices of copper wires the better Mark's profit will be. John will be obligated to buy the copper wire at the strike price, irrespective of its current market price.

This means that this contract is based on speculation of the prices going down.

How does it work?

- The current price of copper wires in the market is $2.75/lb.

- Mark thinks that the prices will drop below $2.5/lb. in the next 60 days.
- John doesn't agree with this drop. He thinks otherwise. He believes that the prices won't drop.
- They both make an agreement. The agreed quantity of copper wire is again 1 Mt. The speculated price is $2.5/lb. John agrees that if the prices drop below this level then Mark can buy this quantity from the open market at a low rate and sell it to him at $2.5/lb. The difference amount will be his profit.
- The premium of this sell or put contract is $200.

A **Put Option** is the guarantee of the seller to buy the predefined stocks (**Lot Size**) at a predefined price (**the Strike Price**), by a predefined date (**Expiration Date**) in lieu of the **Premium.**

If the market price of copper wires doesn't go down at all, the deal won't be sweet for Mark anymore.

He has taken a put option of the stock at the strike price of $2.5/lb., expecting a market price drop. If the price rises, then this contract will be worthless for him. He will have to forgo his premium amount and walk away. John will pocket the premium merrily.

However, if the price of copper wires really goes down, John's losses could be unlimited. Suppose, due to some discovery or invention, the copper wire becomes worthless. Then Mark can happily exercise his put option and ask John to buy the stock and pay the difference. Suppose it starts trading at $0.20/lb. Then John will have to pay the difference amount, coming out to be $2.5-0.2 = $2.3/lb. profit for Mark. It is a higher risk for John as he has everything to lose, whereas the risk for Mark is limited to $200, which he paid in the form of the premium.

Chapter 5

Components of an Options Trade

Let's review the Call and Put Options.

In a call option, you gain from the rise in the price of a stock bought at a predetermined strike price. In a put option, you gain from the fall of a stock price bought at the predetermined strike price. Time is a very important factor here. This is because the expiration date of an option contract is fixed. On the day of the expiration, the contract will become worthless. It means that the premium paid for the contract will become nil for the buyer of the call or put option.

Important things to note from this example:

Strike Price: It is the price at which any commodity is agreed to be bought or sold in the options contract. Beyond the date of the contract, this becomes non-negotiable for the seller. It means he cannot ask for a higher price within the contract at any point in time before the Expiration Date. Even if he has agreed to sell iron bars at a certain price and they suddenly become as precious as gold, the seller will have to settle for the prices agreed earlier.

Premium: It is the price of the contract or the price of the privilege you pay for fixing the price of a commodity for a certain period of time. It is non-refundable or non-adjustable. The buyer of the call or put option will have to pay the full price of the stock, as this amount is non-adjustable in the final amount. In a call or put option contract, your profit or loss will be the increase or decrease in the premium amount.

Expiration date: This is the validity period of the contract. Suppose the buyer enters into a call option contract of 30 days. The price of the particular stock won't rise until the 31st day. It is worthless for the buyer if he hasn't entered into a new contract. The contract will expire on its predecided date. Its expiry is non-extendable in any condition.

Lot Size: The quantity of the stock is also decided at the time of the contract. The buyer cannot ask for more quantity at the same rate if the prices go up and down at a later stage. The conditions of the contract are very clear.

The liabilities of the buyer and the seller of a put contract:

The buyer of the put contract has a limited liability. If the stock doesn't go down as he had expected, he can end up losing all his money invested in the premium amount. This amount is generally very small compared to the actual cost of the stock. This means that the buyer of the put is covered to a great extent.

The seller of the put contract has an unlimited liability. The stock can become practically worthless. There have been companies that have closed up shop all of a sudden. In that case, the seller of the put will have to repay the complete difference amount to the buyer of the put.

The expiration date is very important and it always must be kept in context. Anything happening beyond the expiration date is of no value for both parties in terms of the contract. A stock can underperform or overachieve and the previous buyer of the call or put will have nothing to gain or lose from it. The contract ends on the expiration date.

Chapter 6

Understanding the Moneyness of Options

What is moneyness in an options contract?

Moneyness is the assessment of the advantage an option buyer may enjoy in the market.

It is the comparative analysis of the cash market price with the strike price of the stock in the options market. It reflects whether or not the buyer has any specific advantage.

This is VERY important:

It is essential that you pay special attention to moneyness. It can make or break an options trade. The options trade is a speculative game. Yet, the speculation has to be within limits. You are not sitting blind here. It is about money. Companies don't run on a hunch. Businessmen and corporate houses are managing them. Markets keep assessing them day and night, and the value in the market is based upon that.

A company may be decimated to the ground very fast. But for that to happen, there needs to be some very strong news leading to such a catastrophe. In the same way, if you think that a stock will outperform, then there must be a basis for that. Any big order, positive sentiment in the market, any new product launch underway that will rock the world, anything of this sort.

This assessment of value is called speculating the **moneyness** in any options trade.

On the basis of this advantage, the options contract can be classified into three broad categories:

In the Money (ITM): This is where the strike price gives some specific advantage to the buyer, in comparison to the cash market. The opportunity to earn money from the trade is very high in such situations.

These are the stocks that have a better strike price as compared to their current price in the cash market.

However, you must keep in mind that markets are very volatile. A stock which is currently ***in the money*** may not remain so tomorrow. Still, going for the ITM stocks is a safe strategy. They are usually near their goals; hence the chances of making money from them increase. Their time to target is short, and the time decay affects them the least. These are some of the concepts you'll get to understand in detail later in the book.

At the Money (ATM): In this situation, the strike price of the product or the service remains equivalent to the cash market price. This doesn't give any advantage to the option buyer. The chances to earn money are reduced.

These are the stocks that have strike prices comparable to the prices in the cash market. It means they neither offer you any advantage nor put you in any disadvantageous position. They have a good chance to equally grow or sink.

Out of the Money (OTM): In this situation, the strike price is very far or difficult to achieve in comparison to the price in the cash market. Here, the options buyer is in a very disadvantageous position.

The chances of making money reduce significantly.

These are the options trades where the strike price is significantly far from the current cash market price. It can put you in a tight spot. Such trades need a very sharp eye and the buyer must know the pulse of the market. They, too, have a possibility of earning money. However, you must have solid grounds to go for them. Let us take metals as an example. Suppose you are a metal trader and you know that some specific metal will be in great demand within a set period of time. You use that knowledge and buy the stocks of that metal at a cheap price. If the metal price picks up, then you are bound to earn good money. Trading on such options is risky and should be avoided by beginners. However, as an upside, the premium for such option trades is comparatively very low.

However, before you jump to conclusions about the ITMs, ATMs or the OTMs, there are other things to consider. Always remember the market is a very volatile place. The situations change very rapidly and the moneyness can also change in the same way. A trade that was looking lucrative might turn into a disaster. A trade that was out of the money may start calling the shots. The tides change with every news in the market. A stock getting big news or showing losses in the quarterly balance sheets is likely to attract such rapid changes. It happens all the time. However, a trade in which an OTM is gaining the ITMs for that trade will be gaining big time.

Let's talk about the premium

The premium is the total amount being put at stake in the options trade. Yet, while assessing an option such as ATM, ITM or OTM, you must keep the premium aside. The actual comparison must always be made between the strike price of the call or put option and the price of that stock in the cash market. This doesn't mean the price of the premium isn't important. The calculation of the premium price into this will make things complex for you and may take you towards misleading assessments. Here, your target is to identify whether the stock can reach the strike price and if the strike price is comparable to the cash market price or not. Doing so will make things simpler for you.

The main objective of this classification is to understand the contract clearly and analyze its advantage or disadvantage. It will bring clarity to your mind and also open the risk and reward ratio for understanding.

When you have clearly categorized the options trades as ITM, ATM or OTM, you are in a better position to form your options strategy. It is very important to remember that you must have a strategy. This might look like buying a lottery ticket, but it isn't. You must have plans for doing anything and everything. Moving hastily, exiting from trades without giving a thought or entering into them without a plan can prove very costly.

Last but not least, the price of the premium cannot be a factor while categorizing the options as ATM, ITM or OTM. However, it will be an important factor while you compare the ITM, ATM or OTM stocks of the same category.

Premium is the most important point in an options strategy. It is, and must always remain, your focal point. You must compare the premium of one ITM contract with the premium of another ITM contract. This will help you in choosing the right options trade.

Chapter 7

Assessing the Moneyness in Call Options

Correct assessment of a stock as ITM, ATM or OTM is your objective here. There are various principles working behind these calculations and everyone is trying to win the game. It is your first leg towards making a profit in the market.

We will now move forward with scenarios related to the ABCL pharmaceutical stock.

Scenario 1:

Let's suppose the date of opening the call option is 1st March, 2017 and its expiration date is 30th March, 2017.

The ABCL stock is currently trading at the cash market at the price of $93.

The seller of the put option has placed a strike price of

$88 on the call option and is charging a premium of $10.

Now, this call option is definitely **in the money** as its cash market price is lower than the Strike price.

The buyer of the call option is thinking that the strike price is lucrative as it is below the cash market price of $93. In the next 30 days, the stock may rise and the buyer will profit.

The seller is moving with a different calculation. The seller is thinking that the price of the stock may plummet and reach a level below $88 in the next 30 days. At this point, the buyer may not be interested in buying the stock anymore. The seller would make a neat profit of the $10 premium; hence it would be a profitable trade.

Scenario 2:

Now, suppose the same stock is up for sale. The date is now 5th March, 2017. The price of the stock in the cash market is $91. The premium is $9 and the Strike Price is $87. The ticking time bomb of the expiration date has started and the price has come down a bit as expected by the seller. The figures may have changed slightly, but the trade is still *in the money* because the strike price is lower than the cash market price.

Scenario 3:

Some more days pass. The date is now 10th March, 2017 and the cash market price goes down to $88. The strike price of the call option is $88 and the premium is now at $7. Now, this trade is not offering any advantageous position to the buyer. The strike price and the cash market price are the same. Yet, the stock is not showing any disadvantageous prospects either. The chance of the stock price going up or down is the same. This trade is *at the money*.

Scenario 4:

The date is now 10th March, 2017. The stock hasn't performed well. It now stands at $83 in the cash market. The strike price of the call option is $86 and the premium is $5. Now this trade is getting riskier. It is offering a disadvantageous position to the call buyer. The market price going up from here gets risky but, still being a market component, there are possibilities that the stock might recover. But this trade is now *out of the money*.

Scenario 5:

A few more days pass. The date is now 16th March, 2017. The stock has picked up a bit in the cash market. It is currently trading at $89 in the cash market. The strike price of the trade is $86 with a premium of $6. Now this trade has become ***in the money*** for a new buyer as it is offering an advantageous position. The possibilities of the price going higher as well as giving benefits are rich.

The purpose of these scenarios is to explain the market situations to you clearly. The market is very volatile and dynamic. It doesn't remain the same. It can suddenly change, and the stocks which have been trading lackluster can start shining all of a sudden. The trick is to identify the right time to enter into any options trade.

Chapter 8

Assessing the Moneyness in Put Options

Before we begin understanding moneyness in the put options, it is important that you understand that in the put option, the put buyer will eventually sell the stocks. The put seller is giving a guarantee to buy the stock at an agreed price. In this case, however, you are the buyer whereas the other party is the seller. This is because there is no actual movement of the stock.

The put is a guarantee of the seller that he/she will buy the stocks at a strike price irrespective of the cash market price within the period of the contract. The actual thing being sold here is the privilege to sell the stock at a later date for a predefined price. That is why the person selling the put option will have to buy the stocks, whereas the person who has bought the put option will just sell the put when the strike price is achieved. This role reversal should not be confusing. The put buyer will remain the buyer in this equation, and the put seller will be called the seller, irrespective of their actual roles.

Scenario 1:

Suppose the pharmaceutical stock is trading in the cash market at $73. The month has just begun as it is just 1st April, 2017. The expiry is 30 days ahead. The put seller has fixed a strike price of $79 with a premium of $10. This is a lucrative trade for the put buyer. He can easily sell it for a profit. There are still many remaining days in the month and there is a great possibility that the stock might go further down.

This is clearly an advantageous position for the put buyer. It is an ***in-the-money*** trade for the put option buyer. The seller is thinking that there is a lot of time left before the expiration date; hence the chances of the stock improving its performance are very high. Each party is working with their own calculations.

Scenario 2:

The date is 10th April, 2017. There are still 20 days to go and the stock has improved a bit. It is currently trading at $79. The strike price of the put option is also $79 and the premium is $7. Now, this presents an equal opportunity to the put buyer. The stock can go any side. It can increase or decrease. It is offering a neutral position at the moment. This means that it is currently an **at the money** trade for the buyer.

Scenario 3:

Now, suppose the ABCL pharmaceutical stock is trading at a cash market price of $98. It is now the middle of the month and the expiration date is in 15 days. The strike price of the put is $79 and the premium is $5. This is clearly a disadvantageous position for the put buyer as the likelihood of the stock going so far down is very low. This an **out-of-the-money** trade for the buyer.

Yet, some buyers might want to get it as they believe that the markets will go down by the end of the month and the prices will plummet.

The seller might think that the stock is performing well, and the chances of its strike price going down are less. There is a very small probability that the buyer will come to him to exercise his right to buy, and he can walk away with the paid premium.

Scenario 4

It is now 21st April, 2017. It's only 9 days until the expiration date. The stock has started taking a dip. It has reached a price of $65 in the cash market. The strike price is $79 and the premium is $14. Now, this trade is offering a clear advantage to the put option buyer. He can take advantage of the dip, which will offer better prospects by the end of the month. It is an *in-the-money* trade for the put buyer.

You'd notice that the price of the premium is constantly changing. The main reason for this is the incentive decided by the put seller for taking the risk. Remember, the risks of the put seller are unlimited. If the ABCL stock keeps going down, it can create huge losses for the put seller. This is the amount the put seller charges for balancing out the losses.

Chapter 9

Understanding the Premium

What is the premium?

The premium is the token or reservation amount you need to pay to the option seller to buy a call or put option. It is the price of the guarantee that the option seller gives you to buy or sell the stocks at a later date, at a current fixed price. It is NOT the price of the stock. It is the price of the risk the option seller is taking and also the price of the guarantee. This is the main reason why the premium is non-refundable and non-adjustable.

Why do you need to pay the premium?

The seller is taking a big risk. You are purchasing the buy option for a stock. It is common knowledge that a stock can skyrocket anytime. In that case, the losses of the option seller would be unlimited. If he steps back from his guarantee to buy the stocks at such a high price, your option contract will become worthless. The premium is the price of that risk.

Now, in the case of a put option, the seller guarantees you that he/she will buy the defined quantity of stocks from you at a predetermined price any time before a fixed date. If the stock performs very poorly or becomes worthless, you'll get filthy rich. The option seller of that put will have to pay the complete difference to you. This is the great risk for which the premium is charged as an incentive.

Remember that the seller of the option is taking two risks. First is the risk of the stock price, as it can go up and down anytime. No one has control over these prices. They are regulated by independent market forces. Second, there's the risk of time. You buy a call or put option for a defined time period. In such a volatile market, waiting for such periods of time is like sitting on a ticking time bomb. You have secured your position by giving the premium amount. Your maximum loss can also be the same as that premium amount. In the case of loss, the option seller will have to honor the guarantee. He/she will have to buy the stocks from you at the predefined price irrespective of the current status of the market. It is a big risk for which the premium is taken.

What are the components of the premium pricing?

1. Intrinsic Value: This is the amount of advantage being given with the strike price. If the value of the advantage is nil, then the value of the intrinsic value will also be zero.

For instance, the premium of the in-the-money (ITM) option is higher, while the premium of the out-of-the-money (OTM) option is lower. The option seller charges the advantageous value of the strike price in the form of intrinsic value.

2. Time Value or Extrinsic Value: This is the value of time that is associated with any premium. For better understanding, we will call it the time value in the remaining part.

A call or put option derives its value from these two parts. The premium is the sum of the intrinsic value and the time value.

For a better understanding, these terms will be discussed in detail in the next chapter.

Chapter 10

Understanding Intrinsic Value

Intrinsic value is the advantage offered by the option seller to the buyer, with the strike price over the cash market price.

This is a very important factor in calculating the premium of an option. You must understand that the premium is never calculated by guesswork. It is the value of the risk taken by the option seller.

You must remember that the intrinsic value is only taken when the option contract is ***in the money***. This is the premium charged by the option seller for giving an advantageous position to the buyer. The ATM and OTM option contracts have no intrinsic value as they offer no advantageous position to the call option buyer.

Now let us consider some scenarios.

Scenario 1:

Going back to the ABCL stock, it is now trading in the cash market at a price of $93. The option seller has given a strike price of $83. The premium for buying this call option is $14.

Now let us understand the breakup of the premium value.

The intrinsic value is the difference between the cash market value and the strike price. This means that the cash market value is $93 and the strike price is $83. This means the intrinsic value will be $93-83 = $10. The remaining $4 is for the time value.

Scenario 2:

The cash market price of the ABCL stock is now at $88. The strike price of the stock is $83. The premium of the call option is $9. Following the same computation above, $88-$88 = $5.

The intrinsic value of the call option is $5 and the time value is $4. Both scenarios were **in the money**, hence they have intrinsic value.

Here are two more scenarios to better understand the premium calculations.

Scenario 3:

Suppose the ABCL stock is trading in the cash market at a price of $88.

The strike price given by the option seller here is $88, while the premium being charged is $7.

In this example, the strike price is equal to the price of the stock in the cash market. Hence, the stock is giving no advantage to the buyer. It is an **at-the-money** trade. This stock has nil intrinsic value. The $7 charged by the option seller here is for the time value.

Scenario 4:

Let's say that the ABCL stock is trading at a price of $88 in the cash market.

The strike price given by the option seller is $93. The premium being asked is $5.

In this example, the call option is an out-of-the-money trade. It is offering no advantage to the buyer. The stock may perform well at a later stage and the buyer might earn from it. However, in the beginning, the seller is not giving any advantageous ground to the seller. Therefore, the intrinsic value of the premium is zero, and the $5 being charged here is for the time value.

The same rule applies to the put options.

Scenario 5:

Let's say that the ABCL stock is trading at a value of $88 in the cash market.

The option seller is offering the put option at a strike price of $83 and asking for a premium of $5.

This is a disadvantageous position for the put buyer; hence it is an out-of-the-money trade. The put buyer will have to wait for the market to settle down before he or she can sell their put with some profit. The $5 premium is just for the time value. This put has zero intrinsic value.

Chapter 11

Understanding Time Value or Extrinsic Value

Time value is a very important thing in an options contract whether it is a call or put option. Time will have an important role to play in it. You must keep in mind that, as time passes by, the value of your option contract starts decreasing. On the expiration date, every option will become worthless, no matter what stock you purchased. If there is a positive difference between the strike price and the cash market price, it will be your profit. The degradation in the time value starts from the first day itself. Therefore, time value is very important.

An option contract is like a human being with a known death date. Consider it a medicine with an expiry date written over it. It may be the most expensive medicine in the world, but after reaching its expiration date, it will lose its value. No doctor would administer it, and it may no longer be as effective as it should be. It may also be toxic to the patient.

The same goes for the options contract. It will be toxic to the buyer on the expiration date. They must exercise their option to buy the stock before the expiration date at all costs or forget the options contract and walk away empty-handed.

An important thing to remember:

The farther the expiration date of the contract, the higher the time value will be.

This happens because, with longer time, the option seller is taking a bigger risk. If the time period is 30 days, you have more time to get out of the trade profitably. The market can go in any direction during this period.

If the timeframe is just 15 days, the risk of the option seller decreases by half in comparison to the above scenario, so the time value will decrease.

When the time remaining is just 7 days, the time value will decrease significantly as the time to perform is really low now. The same calculation will proceed further in the same manner.

Chapter 12

Understanding Time Decay

If you want to remain profitable in an options trade, you must have a clear understanding of how the premium works. It is all about the premium. In an options contract, the only thing you are trading in is the premium, everything else is just hypothetical in nature. You will invest in the premium and you will get the profit from the strike price you bought from that amount.

To further explain the importance of premium, let's go back to its components: the intrinsic value and the time value. The intrinsic value gives your options trade an advantageous start, but it only has a limited function. The time value will play a more important role.

The time decreases in value as it passes by. The value of the options contract also decreases with it.

If you fail to understand the premium function as well as the factors that affect it, it might be difficult for you to make money. Gauging the performance of the option and the forces acting upon it is of the utmost importance.

Time is ever moving. It doesn't stop for anyone. You are aging every day. Even the wealthiest man in the world cannot buy an extra day of his youth with all his money in the world. Time doesn't move backward. The same thing goes for time in the options contract.

Time decay begins at the time the contract is fixed. Its expiration comes near with each passing day, whether the intrinsic value goes up or down.

Time decay, however, is not consistent. It definitely happens with every option contract, but the decrease in time value will depend on many factors.

If you currently have an in-the-money trade, you will be earning a profit because the option will have an intrinsic value. However, if you have an out-of-the-money trade, the intrinsic and time value will be zero. This means that your premium is also zero.

As we move closer towards the expiration date of the options contract, time value decreases until it becomes zero on the expiration date.

Aside from time decay, another factor affecting time value is market volatility. At certain points, time value may increase despite the time decay. This happens due to the volatility of the market.

There is no formula to specifically determine the change in time value or predict when the shift in time value happens. Because time value is the estimation of the risk of the option seller, the higher the risk the greater the time value will be.

Let's assume that the call option is about to expire in three days, and yet the prices of the stock are changing rapidly. In that case, the option seller might put a higher time value on the option contract, since the chances of the option contract being an in-the-money trade are higher. This is a great way for the option seller to cover any losses.

To put it simply:

- The greater the intrinsic value of the option contract, the lower the time value would be.
- The lower the intrinsic value of the option contract goes, the higher the option seller charges in the form of time value.

Chapter 13

How an Actual Trade Takes Place

There are several parties involved in a trade. It isn't possible to trade directly with everyone, and it isn't even practical. This is why, for the sake of convenience, stock exchanges were formed. This is a channel where all the stocks are being traded.

You cannot work directly with the stock exchange as this would create great confusion. It would mean too many people making deals at the same time. This is where brokers come into play.

Brokers work as the mediators, as the channel of communication between you and the exchange. They charge a commission for their service. In the stock exchange industry's early stages, most of the transactions were carried out by the brokers on behalf of their clients. Brokers nowadays still carry out transactions on behalf of their clients, but the clients now have the option to manage their accounts easily.

You will have to open a trading account with a broker, and the broker will give you access to that trading account.

Currently, a number of software programs have been successfully developed where you can directly trade on stock exchanges. The program recommendation, as well as the access credentials, will be provided by the brokerage firm you'll choose.

To start a trade, once you're logged in on your trading software, let's use the ABCL stock as a sample product.

Go to the Options menu and choose the product name. You will then see a new window with the following details:

- The segment in which you want to trade.
- The name of the stock you want to trade.
- Your trade options (call or put option).
- The expiration date of the option contract.
- The strike rate of the option. This is the price you believe the stock can reach before the expiration date. Choose it wisely.

- The premium amount. This is the amount being charged by the seller of the options contract to sell you the option.
- The quantity of options you want to buy. Since the options are purchased in a lot of 100 shares, quantity 1 is a bundle of 100 shares, 2 is a bundle of 200 shares and so on, and so forth. The premium will be multiplied by the quantity.

After filling out all the details carefully, you may now place the order. You will also be asked to confirm the quantity you want to buy.

Finally, you will be shown the total premium you'll have to pay for that quantity.

You can set the pricing in two ways:

1. You can send the order at market price. This means you are ready to buy the lot on the current market value. It is important to understand that choosing this option means you will have no control over the price and that there might be a little variation in the final amount. Your order will go to the exchange, and the exchange will match the orders of the buyers and

sellers. Because your order is on the market price, it will quickly get matched with the asking price of the sellers quickly. However, the sellers might also be asking for a higher price, making your order more expensive.

2. You can set a buy price and send the order to the market. This order will be kept in waiting to be matched. Once there are sellers ready to sell at your price, your order will be matched and executed. This is where you'll have complete control over the price of the order but an uncertainty as to whether you will get the trade or not. When some trade is highly in demand, you may not get your order executed because there are other buyers who are ready to buy at a higher price or at the market price.

Once placed, the order goes to the exchange and the orders with the same parameters get matched. You will then receive confirmation once your order gets processed.

You now have the call or put option for the specified period. This means that you now have an open position as well as an idea of the market variations. Whichever way the market moves, your open position will keep showing the product's status in the market.

You can choose to exercise your open position of call or put option at any point within the expiration date and reap a profit. However, if it's done after the expiration date, your order is out of the money, meaning you'll lose your money. If it is in the money, you'll gain from your order.

Let's assume you have a new open position. Your investment is locked and you can only get the increased or decreased amount by closing your position. How do you close an open position?

Here are two ways to close an open position:

1. Wait until the expiration date.

On the expiration date of the options contract, if your option trade is in the money, it will still have intrinsic value. You will get the profit in the form of the premium amount.

You do not have to do anything else. The option trade reaches its expiry, and the trade gets executed automatically. If the trade is out of the money, you may now walk away without your investment. The profit or loss is the difference between the current premium and the initial premium you paid.

2. Don't wait for the expiration date of the option trade.

Watch your trade closely. If possible, find a point where you can reap profit from the trade and square off your position and exit. This is the most common and widely-followed practice. With this choice, the trade might have intrinsic value along with time value in the premium, meaning your chances of exiting with profit may increase.

Closing of positions will be discussed in detail in the next chapter.

Chapter 14

Closing an Open Call or Put Option Position before the Expiration Date

Closing an open call or put option position before the expiration date is similar to short-term trading. Here, you'll make a speculative trade on the assumption that this will pay off.

You wait for some time and watch the market closely.

You encounter 2 scenarios:

1. You feel that the trade is in a position to pay you off if you close it now and it might not perform that well by the expiration date. This is your assumption. You can be wrong and may lose on the better pay-offs that you might get later on. But you are wise and believe that one in the hand is always better than two in the bush.

You wait for the best strike price at which you will get the highest premium and exit the open position by squaring it off.

2. During the time you have entered into this open position, you have been continuously exposed to the market risk. The trade is not performing well and you are losing money. You believe that the call option will become zero as it nears the expiration date. Although you are still losing money on the stock you can still get some part of the money by squaring off your position.

You choose to exit the trade right away, content with the money you get.

Both of these are very probable scenarios. You can either make money on the trade or lose money on it. Exiting at the right time gives you the advantage of getting the benefit of the intrinsic value and time value in the options trade. It is a good strategy if not the best strategy. There is always a chance that the stock may perform quite well in the end. But it is just a chance and there is a strong likelihood the trade might become zero towards the end.

Closing the call option when there is still time to do so before expiry is what we are going to understand here.

In this strategy, the objective is very clear. The objective is to reap the benefits of the ups and downs in the market.

Now let us understand the way a call option position is squared off.

Suppose you had purchased 2 lots of call option for ABCL stock at the strike price of $88 with an expiry of 17th March, 2017.

Now open your trading portal. There, you'll find all the options you hold. Pick the ABCL call option. In the Actions Menu, you'll find four options to select from.

1. Buy to Open

2. Buy to Close

3. Sell to Open

4. Sell to Close

Closing a call options

You have bought the call option of ABCL. To close this position you need to sell this option in the market.

The closing off also works in the same way as purchasing; you can either sell it at the market price or set a rate of yours at which you want to sell your call option.

On the market, the call option will get sold off immediately at whatever the price is available in the market. There is a possibility that you might get a slightly lower rate than you expected. However, the chances are your trade will get sold immediately, depending upon the number of open interests and buyers in the market.

Closing a put option

It works in the same way for put options. Just open the Action menu after selecting your trade. Now choose the 'Buy to Close' option for closing the put option trade. The remaining things work in pretty much the same manner. You just have to remember that you can only earn profits in a put option if you are selling it at a lower price than you bought it for.

One important thing to remember here is that, apart from the profit and loss, you also have to pay the brokerage of the firm with which you have your trading account. The brokerage is generally fixed on the amount and quantity and it is calculated with the taxes at the end of every trade.

Chapter 15

Valuation of Options in the Bullish and Bearish Markets

In the bullish market, the call options gain momentum. The buyers are interested in purchasing the options as they get a guarantee to buy those products at a secured lower price. The seller of the call option also increases the price of the premium as the seller feels that the risk has increased. This also creates a scarcity of the options and high demand. In this case, your call options will gain a higher premium and you can earn profits from them.

However, all the call options gain momentum in the bullish markets yet the movement of all the options is not the same.

Deep ITM Strikes

The call options with Deep ITM strikes hit gold all of a sudden. They are already ripe and ready to give profits. The traders are highly interested in them as the call options offer the convenience to buy the stock at a lower price in a rising market. The traders in the open market would want to enter into such trades even if they had to pay a higher price. The seller of the call option also increases the price of the premium as the risk has increased manifold. He/she would have to sell the goods at a lower price in an outperforming market and would suffer losses. So the increased premium is the security to recover the losses.

The shortage of call option traded from the seller's end and the high demand creates a very favorable space for such call options. The Deep ITM strikes are already ripe as they are the closest to the strike rates or have already achieved them. They would give the maximum benefit.

ITM Strikes

ITM strikes also pay really well in the bullish markets. The sentiments are good and the ITM strikes soon get ripe. They show great momentum. Although they are not able to catch the same benefit of the tide as the Deep ITM strikes yet, they are the second best gainers. You might not see the market momentum getting converted into premium, yet the premiums increase heftily.

ATM Strikes

The premiums of these call options also move fast. They have a high possibility of becoming ITM. They show great progress and promise. The premiums increase rapidly and the call option bearers can gain a good profit. The profits from here decrease rapidly as the options are farther from the strike price and by the time the strike price reaches there the momentum in the stock is lost.

OTM Strikes

Premiums in these options also move fast but fail to capture momentum. The option holder may gain a bit but wouldn't be able to reap the benefits all the way. These option strikes are way too far. However, the premiums increase and the time value will have a positive impact on the prospects.

Deep OTM

Movement is there but the premiums move comparatively slowly. These are very far from the strike price. They move due to the bullish movement in the market, but the movement is just like the displacement from aftershocks once an earthquake has passed.

If the markets are bullish the call options gain rapidly but the put options lose value in the same proportion. Put options become unattractive in the bullish markets. No one is ready to sell their good at a lower contracted price rather than selling them at a higher price in the open market.

Hence, the premiums of the put options decrease rapidly. The traders may lose a big chunk of their money in this tide. However, if the expiry is far then the traders can choose to remain steady in the market and wait for the wave to settle down a bit.

Markets are very volatile and ever-changing. Nothing is permanent in the equity market. The bullish trends settle down pretty quickly and people start selling. So there is always a chance. In options this may work better because exiting at such stages wouldn't give any benefit to the holder of the put option.

The performance of call and put options in bearish markets

If the markets are bearish then the put options gain momentum. The reason is very simple. The prices of the commodities are going down. Through the put contracts, the put seller gives a guarantee to the put buyers to buy the stocks at a pre-agreed high price irrespective of the market price.

When the markets go down, the put option prices become attractive. The put holders can get good money out of them. They can buy the put options at a lower price and sell them to the put seller at a higher price. The difference in the premium is the profit.

Deep in the Money (ITM)

These trades gain the highest as they are already at a ripe price and get the benefit of the complete momentum.

In the Money (ITM)

These trades also get good profit. They are near the strike price; hence they get good momentum.

At the Money (ATM)

These trades have great likelihood of being converted into ITM; hence they see a good gain in the premium.

Out of the Money (OTM)

These are a bit farther from the strike price, but they still gain from the overall market sentiment.

Deep out of the Money (OTM)

These trades have less to gain. Their target price is far, yet they also get the benefit of the wind to some extent. They still have the time value by their side.

The performance of call options in a bearish market

The call options become worthless in the bearish markets as the traders are more interested in reaping the benefits of the downward trend. The call options usually lose their premium amount as no one shows interest in them. However, even exiting them would provide no benefit, so taking them to the expiry is the only option left. If the trend of the market changes somehow, they may recover a bit.

Chapter 16

Understanding Open Interests (OI) in Options

Open interest reflects the strength of the market. It denotes the number of people interested in a particular trade. This is a very important number. Suppose a stock has been rising continuously but there are no open interests in that stock; it may mean that people are losing interest in that stock. You might face a problem with that stock as nothing can keep moving indefinitely without the active participation of the market.

Open interests provide a strong footing to any stock. It doesn't matter whether the stock is falling or rising, a large number of people interested in that stock will keep it alive and kicking in the market.

We can consider 4 scenarios to understand open interests

1. The prices of a particular trade are rising steadily. People are showing interest in that trade. This means the market is strong.

2. If the prices of a particular trade are falling continuously but people are still showing interest in it then it is a bad sign for the market. This will weaken the market and the prices will continue to fall.

3. If the prices of a trade are rising but people are not showing interest in that trade then it shows that the market has started weakening. This is a red flag.

4. If the prices of a particular trade start falling but there is a lack of open interest in that stock then this means the market is strengthening. People are more inclined towards buying than shorting the trades. It is a positive sign.

A good understanding of the open interests in the market will help you in speculating the trend of the market. It is an important factor and will help you in navigating the market safely.

You must understand that your guess cannot be much better than the guess of hundreds of others who are managing this market. The other thing is that the market runs on the sentiments, it doesn't really run on logic. If a thousand people are thinking something will make money then, believe me, it is already making money.

If you want to make money in the opposite market then either you have to be a genius or have some really good backing with a plan.

If you don't have any of these then it is safe to see the mood of the market and act accordingly.

Open interests give power to any stock. They keep the trades alive. Transactions keep ticking.

However, there is also another viewpoint about open interests. Some experts believe that open interests reflect the confidence of the option sellers. If there is any particular option trade that has a great number of open interests, then it wouldn't be hidden from the eyes of the option sellers. Selling a call option is a risk the seller takes. But it is not a blind risk. It is an informed risk. There are several calculations behind it. The seller knows with great accuracy that those levels wouldn't be tested. Otherwise, the losses would become unmanageable. It can happen once in a while, but the same thing occurring repeatedly can ruin any option seller. So, just following the open interests blindly can be very misleading.

The fact of the matter is that open interests reflect the mood of the market. They show that a stock is being actively traded on the stock exchange.

They also show the confidence of the buyers and the sellers on the stock.

Making the final deductions based on these facts will always be your prerogative.

Chapter 17

Understanding the Greeks

The stock market has always been called an uncertain arena and to an extent it certainly is. But have you ever wondered why the big bulls of the market never face the wrath of this uncertainty? How do they manage to prosper year on year while people come and get decimated?

They have no connivance with the insiders. The market is free and flowing. It isn't being controlled by any individual. Yet, some people just keep on making money. To top it all, the options trade is a highly speculative trade. You don't have any commodity in your hand besides a guarantee and you have to pay a price for that guarantee. Yet, some people even make a consistent profit upon that, too, and make profits consistently. Take the options sellers as an example. I couldn't imagine a braver person than an option seller. I would make an equal bet with a person sitting with me. It is risky but, still, I may make it considering the fact that we both have the equal amount to lose. But for a second consider the loss an option seller can face. A stock can just become worthless or start touching the skies. The option seller has to be prepared to deal with it. Yet, they remain rich. They might lose one or two trades here and there, but they are definitely having the last laugh.

Ever wondered how this 'miracle' happens? The secret is the word 'Miracle'. People invest on a hunch in the cash market thinking that things happen by miracle or fluke here. Some even strike beginners luck and get a couple of trades in their favor. But this never goes on forever because they are not taking the stock market investment seriously. This is no miracle. It is pure science and mathematics. You need to study the parameters. Understand the direction of the wind and then jump with a glider in the direction the wind assists you.

This may look to an outsider as though the wind is taking you as a glider doesn't have an engine. But he forgets that the person in the glider is taking advantage of the wind. He has calculated the direction of the wind, the speed, the pressure and the angle he needs to take to reach where he needs to go with the help of the wind.

These parameters in the options market are called the Greeks. As a beginner, you may not realize their importance, but they are very important. By understanding the Greeks and applying them wisely you can make winning trades on a regular basis.

There are 4 very important Greek options:

1. Delta
2. Gamma
3. Theta
4. Vega

These Greeks reflect four important parameters of the market. If you understand their meanings properly and deduce the results reflected by them clearly then your chances of winning will increase considerably.

The Greeks offer you the power of valuable information.

You can guess the shifts in the premium changes.

Greeks can prove to be a tool to predict the quantum of change in the premium.

The Greeks keep changing rapidly themselves. You have to understand their change and its importance.

Chapter 18

Understanding Delta

Delta explains the relationship between the change in cash price of the stock and the change in premium. Delta denotes the proportion in which the change in cash price and premium takes place. If the cash price of a stock rises the premium of the stock option might also increase. But to what extent it will increase is predicted by the Delta.

The formula of Delta is

Change in Premium/Change in Cash Price

If the price of the stock increases by $10 in the cash market and the premium has increased by $5, then your Delta is 0.5.

The Delta ranges between 0 and 1 in call options. It can be any value like 0.1, 0.2, 0.3, etc.

So if the delta for any call option is 0.3 it means that if the stock increases by $10 then there would be an increase of $3 in the premium.

The Delta for put options is negative. It ranges from 0 to -1.

Why understanding Delta is important

We know that options trading is all about premium. Before you invest in any stock it is important to know the kind of change you'll see if the prices go north or south. You would want your premium to increase as it will maximize your profits. So scrutinizing the Delta before you invest in the options trade is important for you.

Delta Ranges for Call Options

For the deep-in-the-money (ITM) call options the Delta value is near 1. But as it progresses down the lane towards the deep out of the money (OTM) the Delta value lingers in the lower brackets near 0.1.

Delta Ranges for Put Options

The Delta value for put options is negative. The better the position of the put option is the higher the delta range would be.

Chapter 19

Understanding Gamma

We now understand that Delta shows the rate by which the change in the cash price of any stock would affect the price of the premium. It is important to understand Delta as it affects your overall profit or loss from the trade.

However, the value of Delta is also not static. This means when the markets change rapidly, the value of Delta also changes accordingly. Suppose the markets are positive so your call option would appreciate. If you have an out-of-the-money trade the change in its premium is slow. But it wouldn't remain the same forever. If the markets are rising fast then the OTM trade can become an ITM and the Delta would also increase.

The premium, which was increasing at a rate of 0.3, might start increasing at a rate of 0.6.

Gamma denotes this change in the Delta. It explains the acceleration in the Delta values. It is important that, when a significant change starts taking place in the stock, you keep a close watch on the Gamma and Delta as they will rapidly expose your position. Your profit or loss will increase with the change in the values of Gamma and Delta.

The value of Gamma is derived by the following calculation:

Change in the Value of Delta/Change in Cash Price of the Stock

Knowing the Gamma will help you in understanding how fast the premiums can change for any stock.

Chapter 20

Understanding Theta

Theta explains one of the most important aspects of any options trade and that is the time value or the extrinsic value.

We know that as any options trade moves towards the expiration date, the risk involved increases significantly. But we also know that time value is not static for any trade. It keeps fluctuating as per the performance of the stock. It decays all right, but the decay is not steady. The value can increase or decrease suddenly.

Theta explains the risk involved with respect to the time decay in the options trade. So, if you have a call option with an expiration date of 90 days you'd want a low Theta risk.

Theta explains to us the change in premium with respect to a one-day change in the expiration date.

Some important things to understand about Theta:

Theta will always be negative. It denotes degradation in the value of the premium; hence it can never be positive. It is a value of the time and the time is continuously reducing the options trade. So, Theta will be negative for both call and put options.

It is a Greek that works in favor of the option seller. For the option buyer the Theta is always a negative attribute. The higher the Theta is the greater the risk of the buyer will be.

It is a very important value. It denotes the degradation of your option with each passing day. It means that, whatever the value of Theta is, it will be deducted from the value of your option trade the next day. The premium will decrease by that amount the next day. If you are considering maintaining your position for the next day in the trade, then you must have a close look at the Theta value. It will give you a great insight. You might be expecting a smaller increase in the premium, but the degradation caused by the Theta the very next day might be higher. It is a definite prediction of the loss in value of the premium.

The Theta values are the highest in the ATM trades, the reason for this being that the time value is the highest in the ATM trades and that's why the erosion is also the highest in these trades.

The Theta as an options trade will increase as the trade reaches its expiration.

One of the biggest false assumptions option buyers have is that if the stock keeps increasing the premium will also keep increasing. It doesn't happen this way. The beginners ignore the time erosion caused by the Theta in the value of the premium.

For instance, we take the ABCL stock once again.

The call option stands at $93. The markets are going strong and you have a basis to believe that the stock might rise by a certain value in the next 10 days. But, if you fail to consider the erosion caused by the Theta in the premium then even after the premium rises by those points you will have no gain and might also lose the money in the premium.

Theta will cause mandatory erosion in the value of the options trade with each passing day. The premium will decrease by those many points each day. If the premium is not increasing at a greater pace then you will end up losing money. Napoleon once said, "I can lose a battle but not a minute." The day he lost that minute he had to face the defeat of Waterloo. In the same way, wasting time in an options trade when you do not have any reason to believe that it will rise significantly can prove costly for you.

It's very important to understand Theta value. It is the definite decay in the value of the premium.

If you are a beginner then you must understand the value of Theta in the trade and always keep it at the back of your mind when forming a strategy. Fooling around and wasting time will cause decay in the premium and you might end up losing money.

Chapter 21

Understanding Vega

Vega is a measure of volatility in the market. It shows the change in the premium of an option with regard to its change in volatility.

This means that for 1% change in volatility of the option the impact on the option price is reflected by Vega.

Vega = Change in Premium/1% Increase in Volatility

It reflects that the premium would also increase with the same ratio when the volatility in the stock increases by 1%. It is an important Greek to follow when you see any fluctuation in the market. It predicts the change in the premium amount with the change in the prices of the stock.

Some important facts about Vega

Vega is the highest in at-the-money (ATM) trades. Vega reflects the volatility and these stocks see the highest volatility in the case of any market shift. This is the reason why the Vega is the highest in ATM trades.

Time value in the options trade affects Vega acutely. The higher the time value in any options trade the greater the value of Vega will be.

Conclusion

Thank you for making it through to the end of this book, let's hope it was informative and able to provide you with all of the tools you need to achieve your goals whatever they may be.

Options trading is a great way to enter the market with a small amount of capital. The premiums keep changing and you can make a lot of money if you trade wisely and do not take unnecessary risks.

This book has explained all the important facts about the options trade. It has tried to throw light on all the aspects of options trading so that you understand the functioning of the market. Trading is just a psychological game. Both parties are trying to guess the direction of the wind. The seller is taking a bigger risk but the profit of the seller is also sturdy as the seller is an experienced player. You have to understand the psyche of the seller.

Knowledge is power when it comes to trading. It is not a guessing game. You are speculating about the rates and the way the market will behave, yet you must have a plan and reasoning behind the actions. Once in the trade, this knowledge will help you in figuring the market will move and the kind of profits you can expect to make.

The Greeks explained in the last few chapters are of great significance and they help you in understanding your risks. The biggest mistake new traders make is not calculating the real value hidden in the trade. A contract that may look attractive might not have any real value at all. You must pay special attention to that part.

The aim of this book is to explain the main concepts of options trading and how it works. You will have to form strategies to move into the market and you will definitely make a profit.

Finally, if you found this book useful in any way, a review on Amazon is always appreciated!

www.ingramcontent.com/pod-product-compliance
Lightning Source LLC
Chambersburg PA
CBHW031630210526
45464CB00004B/1839